# "Not to Reason Why"

D1736827

A Sailor's Letters Home About Life
Aboard the Battle-Scarred USS WASP
During World War II

Former Midshipman
## Warren I. Jaycox, Ed.D.

Chronicling the Letters of

## Perrin B. Heaverin, Jr.,
former Seaman First Class

White Cottage Publishing Company
Trinidad, Colorado

Published by
# White Cottage Publishing Company
http://whitecottagepublishing.com

Interior and Cover Design: Tom Mack, MBA
# White Cottage Publishing Company

The title of this book comes from the famous poem: "The Charge of the Light Brigade" by The Right Honorable Alfred, Lord Tennyson (1817-1904), written in 1854.

Additional copies of this book can be ordered from your favorite bookseller. Bulk orders of this book can be ordered from the publisher.

To contact the author via E-mail: warren.jaycox@whitecottagepublishing.com

Printed in the United States of America for Worldwide Distribution
ISBN: 9798415651764

# Dedication

To the memory of the officers, enlisted men and personnel of attached air groups who served aboard the *USS WASP* (CV-18) during World War II.

# Acknowledgments

It was the brave, patriotic young men like Perrin Heaverin, Jr., who put their lives on the line in defense of their country... who inspired the writing of this book. The core of this book is the many letters Seaman First Class Heaverin wrote to his Mom and "Pop" during his time in the Navy. He wrote most of them while he was part of the crew of the *USS WASP*, an aircraft carrier that was involved in the many of the decisive naval battles in the Pacific Theater of World War II.

These letters, saved by Perrin's parents, were loaned to this author and formed the basis for this book. He also gave this author information about the *USS WASP* consisting of an official Navy document that details the history of the *USS WASP* from birth to the end of World War II. He wrote, or is responsible for a significant portion of the book.

Putting a book together is more than just writing and printing. It takes an editor like Tom Mack, who has the knowledge and skill to bring a book to fruition. Tom Mack excels in this area and has stuck with the project, not because that's what he does, but because he believes in the project. It is a story that reflects the solidifying values of this great country. The dedication of Tom Mack continued this faith throughout his bout with heart issues, eventual open-heart surgery, and subsequent cardiac rehabilitation. I am forever thankful to him for his intense efforts to see this book finally off the press.

I also appreciate the efforts of Perrin's nephew: David Lofftus and his wife Sylvia. They shared their knowledge, access to family history, and lifelong contact with Uncle Buddy. In the interest of full disclosure, this author's late wife: Jeanette (nèe Woods) Jaycox, was Uncle Buddy's niece. I guess that makes me a "nephew-in-law." As such, It has been my pleasure and honor to attend several *U.S.S. WASP* reunions and participate in many conversations with Uncle Bud and his shipmates.

I am also indebted to those who reviewed and critiqued this book to make it more readable and accurate, including my literary consultant: Ardath MacDonald.

I also want to thank CDR. John Meyn, USNR (Ret.) for taking his time to review the proofs along with the many others who also believed in this project, and who encouraged and assisted me in many ways. God bless you all. You know who you are!

# Preface

On that fateful day, December 7 1941, the thundering rumble of hundreds of Japanese aircraft disrupted what was otherwise a peaceful, sunny, Sunday morning at Honolulu, then the Territory of Hawaii. Bombs exploded on the warships and installations of Pearl Harbor. These aircraft had appeared from over the horizon, surprising everyone. Destruction rained down on the battleships of the United States Navy fleet moored in the harbor. The rat-a-tat of the planes' machines guns echoed off the hillsides behind the harbor as any possible target was attacked. A significant part of the Navy's strength was destroyed that day. The nation was in shock.

Photo from Pearl Harbor Attack

It was that infamous attack that started World War II in the Pacific for the United States of America. It also initiated events that eventually led to the joining of the two main characters of this book: The *USS WASP (CV-18)* whose keel was yet to be laid, and Perrin B. Heaverin, Jr., a young man who was yet to graduate from high school. But I'm getting ahead of the story...

I want to emphasize at this point, that this tome is not intended to be a yet another definitive history of the United States Navy during World War II in the Pacific Theater of Operations. There are a considerable number of well-researched books and articles have covered that subject far better that I could ever imagine doing at this point in my life. So, what is the intellectual, psychological and emotional

Seaman Perrin "Buddy" Heaverin, Jr.

rationale for these many pages? Well, as the late famous radio commentator and personality Paul Harvey was famous for saying, "Now for the rest of the story..."

This book is a composite story of three **Lives**. One **Life** is an individual, another **Life** is a ship, and the third **Life** is a nation.

The individual is Perrin B. Heaverin, Jr. We learn about his life through memories of relatives, and his personal stories of his life through his later recollections; especially by the way of the letters he wrote to his parents: Mom and Pop while aboard the aircraft carricr *USS WASP*.

In a sense, this book is autobiographical, since Perrin (Buddy) Heaverin, Jr. wrote portions of this book. However, within his family, he was called "Buddy." That is how he signed his letters (most of the time). Thankfully, his parents saved and shared them with other family members.

The second **Life** is the *USS WASP* (CV-18) This was the ninth United States Navy ship to bear that name. We learn about the *USS WASP* through excerpts from the ship's log, a record that all ships must keep accurately and timely, sort of a biographical record. The basic resource was an official Navy document, *A History of the USS WASP (CV-18) from 24 November 1943 - 2 September 1945*. After the war, we relied upon other documents and records, such as, *U.S. Navy Fact File: Aircraft Carriers CV-18 USS WASP*. It is Buddy's "home away from home" for over two years.

*USS WASP* **During the War**

Then there is the **Life** of National Will: That **Life**, the support of the people at home that needed be maintained to if the United States was to achieve ultimate victory in World War II. (This was missing in the Vietnam and Korean conflicts, for example). The United States was involved in this war, on three fronts: the war against Germany and Italy in Europe, the war against the Japanese in the Pacific, and the war on the Home Front, a national effort to rally the civilian population to support psychologically, physically, and financially, the needs of the soldiers and sailors on the battlefield while enduring the hardships on the "home front." This is described through posters obtained from archives and personal collections, stories from a few people still alive who can recall civilian existence during the war years, and Buddy's collection of artifacts such as gas stamps, ration books, personal and Navy photographs, and countless Google queries, both on the part of me and also my editor: Tom Mack.

Your author was an eyewitness to this phase of the war effort. Interspersed throughout the text are snippets of recollections of the war as seen through the eyes and inquiring mind of a boy from the aged nine through fourteen. My most vivid memory is the day I was helping my father set up the Christmas Lionel Model Trains in our basement. Suddenly my mother hollered down to us, "Milton, come quick!" He dashed upstairs, and when he didn't return, I joined them. I found my mother sobbing over the console radio, She had just heard the broadcast about the Japanese attack on Pearl Harbor. Mom prayed with us for the safety of her sister who lived on the hillside overlooking the harbor at Honolulu with her Navy husband and three children.

I also recall a time in 1942 when my family was traveling in Massachusetts from Boston to Cape Cod for a nice afternoon on the beach. On the way, we could see the Bethlehem Steel Shipyards in Quincy. We looked at the huge hulk of the ship's hull, that would discover later to be the *USS WASP*. Little did I realize that someday, over 80 years later, I would be writing a book chronicling the activities of the *USS WASP*.

From 1943-1945, I was confined to complete bed rest, a result of the Rheumatic Fever I contracted while in grade school. I would listen on the radio to the newscasts (No television in those days) and read the daily accounts of the War published in the *Baltimore Sun*. My family also subscribed to *Life Magazine*, which arrived weekly. I devoured every picture and read every word. As young boys sometimes do, I kept a scrapbook complete with maps of Europe and the Pacific Ocean. Each day, I would color in the areas the sections that were under allied control. I still have that scrapbook.

Every family was affected by the war in some way. My Uncle Lester (a Lieutenant Commander in the Navy) was at Pearl Harbor when the Japanese mercilessly attacked on that infamous Sunday morning. There were anxious days and weeks until we got news that his wife and three children were safely evacuated from Hawaii and to safety on U.S. soil for the remainder of the war. My Uncle Cecil was called back to the Army Air Force and served in Europe. Our next door neighbor was called into the Navy. My future wife's Uncle Jim served in the Army in the Pacific, and her Uncle Bud enlisted in the Navy — He is a **Life** in this book. Many people do not remember this, but during the War, Blue Star flags would hang in many windows signifying a family member was in the military service. A gold star meant that a family member had paid the ultimate sacrifice!

Whenever my wife and I would visit Uncle Bud, we would eventually hear some tales of his life in the Navy. One day he went to a bookshelf that seemed to be a repository of his memorabilia of the war. He came back with an old manila envelope. That envelope contained all of the letters he had written to his mother and father while he was in the Navy. I read through them and exclaimed that it would make a good book. He was kind enough to let me borrow them so I could scan them and include them in this book. He also let me borrow another book that I used as a source document for many of the facts in this book along with excerpts from the ship's log: *A History of the USS WASP (CV-18) - 24 November 1943 - 2 September 1945*, as mentioned previously.

An attempt is made to weave these two biographies of Bud's life as told in his letters, and the WASP's life as told in the ships log. By reading these two at the same time, one can get the sense of what was really happening. The events described were occurring at about the same time. For example, Buddy would write, "Been pretty busy today." when the log reveals the Ship was under *kamikaze* (Japanese suicide piloted aircraft) attack a just few hours before.

To help readers get the full meaning of Buddy's letters, the original letter  is reproduced on one page with a typed copy provided to help readers in those places where they might think Buddy's writing is hard to read. The typist made some adjustments in the prose to help the reader understand what the letter was trying to say. These are judgment calls, so don't be too harsh or critical of the transcriptionist.

Through his shipboard letters, we get a sense of almost his unceasing boredom when he was not doing his daily duties or the heavy lifting that comes from preparing the *USS WASP*'s planes for frequent, sometimes hourly missions of defense and destruction against the Japanese. The *USS WASP* participated in eight major naval and air battles in the Pacific Theater of Operations.

These letters were written on the paper he had available to him: sometimes it was USS WASP stationery, other times, it was "V-Mail" or just plain paper. Seaman Heaverin was obliged to write his letters with whatever writing instrument was available to him at the time: many times, it was pencil as they were more readily available, but sometimes, it was black, blue, or sometimes even red ink from a fountain pen. Why not ballpoint pen? Here's why: even though the first patent for a ballpoint pen was issued in 1888, very few ever reached the market outside of Argentina until after the War.

Note that Buddy's letters were written on one side of the paper only! That was a War Department standard, so that all letters home from military personnel could be evaluated and censored to eliminate information that might be of value to the enemy... should these letters be captured. We see this in Buddy's letters once in a while, as the reader will notice either the word "CENSORED" over a word or phrase in the letter or even a rectangular hole in the paper where the words were cut out. That means the censors did their duty and cut out some words that they determined might be helpful to the Japanese, should one of the Navy's mailbags fall into their hands.

To give closure to the emotional side of his existence, his thoughts, in retrospect are included in the book. Keep in mind that a popular item in the Navy Exchange is emblazoned with "**Retired** — T*he older we get, the better we were!*" So, if some of their tales are full of hyperbole... **they earned it!**

Sadly, today, there are still young men and women who are separated from their loved ones, sometimes in hazardous and yes, even fatal circumstances. They deserved and got our support then, let's make sure they get that support now!

Warren Jaycox, Ed.D,
former Midshipman,
Colonel, USMCR, Retired
Sonoma, CA

App. not Req.

**Prepare in Duplicate**

Local Board No. 206    91
Los Ang....    037

DEC 9 - 1943    206

Room 5, Central School,
Alhambra, 2, California

(LOCAL BOARD DATE STAMP WITH CODE)

December 9, 1943
(Date of mailing)

## ORDER TO REPORT FOR INDUCTION

The President of the United States,

To     **Perrin**                                       **Heaverin**
          (First name)                            (Middle name)                            (Last name)

Order No.    **12,377-A**

*GREETING:*

Having submitted yourself to a local board composed of your neighbors for the purpose of determining your availability for training and service in the land or naval forces of the United States, you are hereby notified that you have now been selected for training and service therein.

You will, therefore, report to the local board named above at **29 S. Second St. Alhambra, Calif.**
                                                                    (Place of reporting)

at    **6:45**    **a.m.**, on the    **Twenty-first**    day of    **December**          , 19 **43**
   (Hour of reporting)

This local board will furnish transportation to an induction station. You will there be examined, and, if accepted for training and service, you will then be inducted into the land or naval forces.

Persons reporting to the induction station in some instances may be rejected for physical or other reasons. It is well to keep this in mind in arranging your affairs, to prevent any undue hardship if you are rejected at the induction station. If you are employed, you should advise your employer of this notice and of the possibility that you may not be accepted at the induction station. Your employer can then be prepared to replace you if you are accepted, or to continue your employment if you are rejected.

Willful failure to report promptly to this local board at the hour and on the day named in this notice is a violation of the Selective Training and Service Act of 1940, as amended, and subjects the violator to fine and imprisonment.

If you are so far removed from your own local board that reporting in compliance with this order will be a serious hardship and you desire to report to a local board in the area of which you are now located, go immediately to that local board and make written request for transfer of your delivery for induction, taking this order with you.

*N. S. Farrell*
*Member or clerk of the local board.*

U. S. GOVERNMENT PRINTING OFFICE   16—18271—5

D. S. S. Form 150
(Revised 1-15-48)

Copy of Perrin Heaverin's Induction Order

# Table of Contents

# Table of Contents

# Introduction

# Perrin "Bud" Burriss Heaverin, Jr.

## Biography - Part I

Perrin B. Heaverin, Jr. was born on September 20, 1925 in a small maternity hospital in Alhambra, California, not far from his parent's home on Second Street. He was named for his father, Perrin Burriss Heaverin. The name Burriss was his paternal grandmother's maiden name.

Drawing of the SS Mongolia by Fred Pansing

As a young girl of 16, his mother Jamima (Mima) Russell left her home in Lithglow Parish, West Lothoian County, Scotland, crossed the Atlantic Ocean on the passenger ship the *SS Mongolia*, officially immigrated at Ellis Island then traveled by train to California to stay with her sister. His father came to California from Salt Lick Valley, Vanceburg, Lewis County, Kentucky. Buddy was preceded in birth by three sisters: Ruth, Jean, and Hazel. Buddy commented,

> It was difficult being the youngest member of the family especially with three older sisters, or maybe it was easier being the baby, a boy, and all.

Buddy had loving parents, but they didn't always see eye to eye with each other, or with him, especially his mother. His parents were not living together, which is why he wrote separate letters to each of them.

He started his education at Central Elementary School in Alhambra, California. As Buddy said,

> One day I came home from kindergarten and was telling the family about our new "kinder band." Some of the kids beat on the drums, others clapped blocks and the teacher played the piano. Mom asked what I played? I answered, "Nothing, I just stand on a box and waved a stick." I wanted to beat a drum. I had to have it explained to me that I had talent.

Childhood was an active and adventurous time for Buddy. He later wrote,

> One of my earliest vehicles was a tricycle. Every so often I picked a few lemons and carried them in a small bucket on my trike to neighborhood customers. Probably the money from my enterprise came very close to causing my demise and the trike a pile of twisted junk. Billy Bough, a friend, had a tricycle too and he and I were on our way to buy candy at the little store over the railroad tracks on Fourth Street. An express train was coming down the tracks. I said, "Come on, Bill we can make it!" His answer was drowned out by the blast of the trains whistle. It didn't look as though the train was coming very fast or that was it very close. WRONG! I could feel the hot steam on the back of my neck as it whizzed past. I almost lost the race of my young life. I kept it a secret from the folks for fear of getting a spanking. I have great respect for trains; that day I learned a valuable lesson. Pop always wanted me to play catch with him. Come to think of it, the big problem was that all we had was a hard ball and it hurt. Why didn't he buy me a catcher's mitt? We could've had fun.

As he got older he attended Roosevelt Junior High School in Glendale and took on more responsibility, including learning to drive. He explained,

> Mom could drive our new Model A Ford but didn't really enjoy it. One day, we were going someplace and I proved to be an excellent backseat driver. We were slowing due to an uphill grade and the car didn't seem to be running right to me, so I said, "Time to shift, Mom." Those instructions and my irresistible lisp got ol' Lizzie up the hill.

Buddy was an industrious youth, accepting responsibility and learning valuable lessons he would use later in his life. He later recalled,

> I used to work with Pop at the poultry market. My job was to feed the chickens, "candle" the eggs, and pluck the feathers. He would deliver in the afternoon and I would stay and tender store and answer the phone. When I was 16-years-old, I got a job selling Good Humor Ice Cream from a bicycle with a large freezer box built on the front. I was working summers and weekends and still going to school. I eventually came in possession of Pop's old car, the same one I gave the lesson to Mom on how to "shift." I was then 16 years old and the car was thirteen. The car was near it's end, but it was the one I learned to drive on. It was a sad day when it went to the junkyard.

When the Japanese bombed Pearl Harbor on December 7, 1941, Buddy was barely 16 years old. Yet, in a little more than two years, while he was still a student in Alhambra High School, he received his induction notice. The Selective Service System no longer considered educational status once a young man became 18. Put very succinctly: he was 18 and his country needed him. He had to enlist or be drafted into the Army or the Marines. Bud said later,

I chose the Navy because I thought there would be no dust, mud, or marching. When I got to Boot Camp in San Diego, I was fooled.

In his letters home, he describes his new life in the Navy: the regulations, the rigorous structure, and the sometimes intense training. It must have been quite an adjustment of lifestyle and attitude. But Buddy was a survivor. He weathered the challenge.

# Chapter One

## You're in the Navy Now!

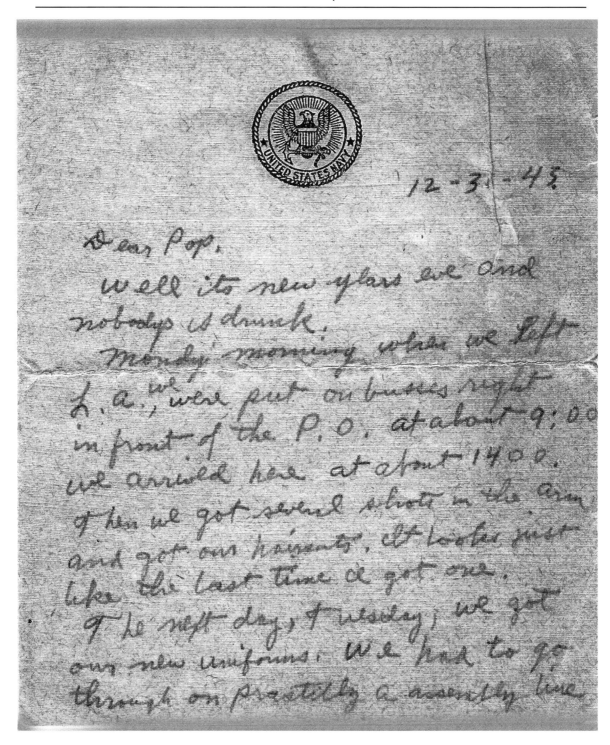

12-31-45

Dear Pop,

Well its new years eve and nobodys is drunk.

Monday morning when we left L.A., we were put on busses right in front of the P.O. at about 9:00 we arrived here at about 1400. Then we got several shots in the arm and got our haircuts. It looked just like the last time I got one.

The next day, Tuesday, we got our new uniforms. We had to go through on practilly a assembly line

getting one thing at a time and
running as we were pushing them on.
After all ours were marked with
our names were put on trucks and
taken to another part of the camp about
2 miles away. We have to stay
here for three weeks and cannot
have any liberty. That is why
I have not written sooner, because
I had no paper. One man from
each hut can go to the canteen and
buy things for all the rest.

We are in small huts or half
tent things 12 men in each. The
canvas sides are rolled up in the day
time.

When it rains we do not go out

but when not we work almost all the time.

Today we took tests almost all day, and I think tomorrow or the next day. Last night and tonight we scrubbed our clothes. We have no clothes pins but have to tie them up with ropes, each a certain way and each string tied up until there is none left.

When I sent my old clothes home I had to send that bag too. I don't know if we can have it back or not.

I have to get up in the middle of the night tonight to go on guard duty.

We keep our clothes in a big canvas bag and whenever we want anything we have to dump it out and scratch for it.

My address here for writing to
me is CO 574, U. S. Naval Training
Station, San Diego 33 Calif.
at the end of our three weeks in
boot camp we will get a liberty of
12 hours. our next liberty is for 2 or
3 days I think.

Well how about you
writing a letter to me you old
goat.

December 31, 1943

Dear Pop,

Well it's New Year's Eve and nobody's drunk.

Monday morning when we left Los Angeles, we were put on buses right in front of the Post Office at about nine o'clock. We arrived here at about 1400. Then we got several shots in the arm and got our haircuts. It looks like the last time I got one.

The next day, Tuesday, we got our new uniforms. We had to go through in like an assembly line getting one thing at a time and running as we were putting them on. After all, ours were marked with our names. (We) were put on trucks and taken to another part of the camp about 2 miles away. We have to stay here for three weeks and cannot have any liberty. That is why I have not written sooner because I had no paper.

One man from each hut can go to the canteen and buy things for all the rest. We are in huts or half-tent things, 12 men in each. The canvas sides are rolled up in the daytime. When it rains we do not go out but when not (raining) we work about all the time.

Today we took tests about all day and I think tomorrow or the next day. Last night and tonight we scrubbed our clothes. We have no clothes pins but have to tie them up with ropes in a certain way, each string tied up until there is none left. When I sent my old clothes home I had to send that bag too. I don't know if we can have it back or not.

I have to get up in the middle of the night tonight to go on guard duty. I keep our clothes in a big canvas bag and whenever we want anything, we have to dump it out and scratch for it.

My address here for writing to me is C0 574 U.S. Naval Training Station. San Diego, 33 Calif.

At the end of our three weeks in Boot Camp, we will get a liberty of 12 hours. Our next liberty is for two or three days, I think.

Well, how about you writing a letter to me, you old goat.

Unsigned

# Sample Training Schedule for Week Three

During week three, recruits begin the physical transformation from recruit to sailor as they learn the basics of uniform presentation and inspection, academic learning, knot tying, the Chain of Command, the Eleven General Orders of the Sentry and military drill and ceremonies.

- You'll learn basic first aid and self-care.
- You'll also learn ship nomenclature, semaphore (flag signaling), and so much more while on the training ship.
- In the classroom, you'll learn about military citizenship and ethics. And you'll be learning about the laws of armed conflict.
- The fun part is where you'll learn how to identify Navy ships and aircraft (a very serious part of their training).
- Finally, you'll learn the basics of seamanship that you will carry on throughout the rest of your Navy career.
- Your first physical evaluation (or PT) will fall on Week 3.
- You will be tested on everything from push-ups, sit-ups, and a timed one and a half mile run.
- Being evaluated for your physical fitness will be a regular thing from here on out.

**Naval Recruits Arriving at Reception Station**

# Chapter Two

## The Bitter Realities of Training

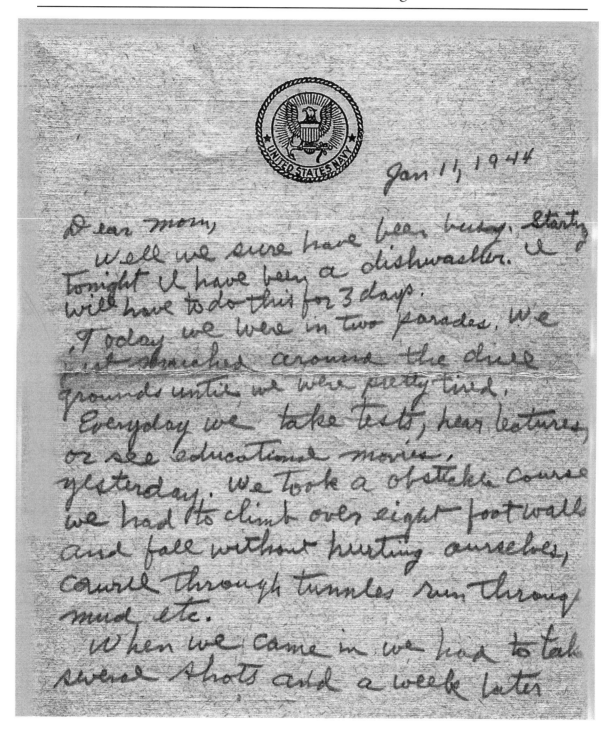

Jan 1, 1944

Dear mom,

Well we sure have been busy. Starting tonight I have been a dishwasher. I will have to do this for 3 days.

Today we were in two parades, We just marched around the drill grounds until we were pretty tired.

Everyday we take tests, hear lectures, or see educational movies.

Yesterday, We took a obstacle course we had to climb over eight foot walls and fall without hurting ourselves, crawl through tunnels run through mud etc.

When we came in we had to take several shots and a week later

. We do almost a days work just working out of that bag, because we have to change clothes so many times a day. Now it will be even harder because we will put on our "whites" to work in the kitchen, then our blues to drill then our whites for lunch, our shorts for exercises etc.

We have learned to send signal by flags. We all must learn that. The other day we took a swimming test.

Our first three weeks we; live in these little cold huts, & then we will move into larger barracks. We had the opportunity to take out insurance so I got $10,000 the most I could get. I am enclosing the policy.

Our first liberty will be after our three weeks detention. But we have to stay in San Diego.

take another double one, we still have to take two more then we will be finished.

We have to get up at 5:00 AM and it sure is cold in these small huts.

Nearly everybody in our outfit has colds.

We have to wash our own clothes that is one job I don't especially like we do not use clothes-pins but have to tie them up with ropes in special knots.

I asked Hazel to send me some fruit cake, I hope I get it.

Will you please send me some cake or cookies? I dont want candy we can buy plenty of that.

We keep our clothes in a canvas bag usually what we want is way down on the bottom, and we have to dig or scratch to find it.

Well I cant think of anything
more to say, so I had better
go to bed. I have to get up early
in the morning.

please write soon, my address
is CO. 43-574 U.S. N.T.S.
San Diego 33 Calif.

love Buddy

January 11, 1944

Dear Mom,

Well, we sure have been busy. Starting tonight, I have been a dishwasher. I will have to do this for three days. Today we were in two parades. We just marched around the drill grounds until we were pretty tired.

Every day we take tests, hear lectures, or see educational movies. Yesterday we took the obstacle course. We had to climb over 8-foot walls and fall without hurting ourselves, crawl through tunnels, run through mud, *etc*. When we came in, we had to take several shots and a week later take another double one. We still have to take two more then we will be finished.

We have to get up at 5 o'clock and it sure is cold in these small huts.

Nearly everybody in our outfit has colds.

We have to wash our own clothes, that is one of the jobs I don't especially like. We do not use clothes pins but have to tie them up with ropes in special knots.

I asked Hazel to send me some fruit cake, I hope I get it. Will you please send me some cake or cookies? I don't want candy; we can buy plenty of that.

We keep our clothes in a canvas bag. Usually what we want is way down on the bottom and we have to dig or scratch to find it.

We do almost a day's work just working out of that bag because we have to change clothes so many times a day. Now it will be even harder because we will put on our whites to work in the kitchen, then our blues to drill, then our whites for lunch, our shorts for exercise, etc.

We have learned to send signals by flags. We all must learn that. The other day we took a swimming test.

Our first three weeks we live in these little cold huts. Then we will move into a larger barracks.

We had the opportunity to take out insurance so I got $10,000, the most I could get. I am enclosing the policy.

Our first liberty will be after our three weeks detention, but we have to stay in San Diego.

Well, I can't think of anything more to say, so I had better go to bed. I have to get up early in the morning.

Please write soon, my address is CO 43–574, U.S.N.T.S., San Diego 33 California.

Love,

Buddy

**Parade Ground at the Training Center**

# Chapter Three

## Drill and Ceremonies... and Marching

In this letter, it is clear that Bud is deeply embedded into Navy Basic Training. He complains, as most sailors do, about having to perform KP. It seems he has drawn the job of washing dishes, a job made harder because they did not have automatic dish-washing machines in World War II.

We know Bud is still early in his Basic Training "Cycle" because they are spending a lot of time on the parade ground learning to march to cadence and to perform the various marching maneuvers.

World War II is also the first war where soldiers and sailors started receiving immunization shots in the hope they would not catch the many diseases that afflict the tropics but are uncommon in the United States.

Unlike today, banking for sailors was a more difficult proposition. They were obliged to send their money home and have members of their family do their banking for them (something modern banking laws would not permit today). However, when it came payday, the sailors would line up and one-at-a-time, say to their Pay Officer,

"Sir, Seaman _____ reports for pay."

The Pay Officer would then look the sailor up on the pay list, confirm their pay, and then count the cash money out to the sailor.

Jan 13, 1944

Dear Mom,

I got a letter from Hazel and one from Jean yesterday and a box of candy from Pop today

I have two checks enclosed that I want you to put in the bank for me.

We may get off for 36 hours instead of 12 on our first liberty. This will be if we are the cleanest company. Both yesterday and today we were the cleanest. I sure hope we win cause then I could come home for a day.

I think I told you that we were on dish washing detail for two days. We are all through with that now. We took two more shots this afternoon, one in each arm. I just got through washing my clothes. The whites that I was wearing when doing dishes were pretty moldy.

I scrubbed on them for about a half an hour, but they still were tattle tale gray.

Tomorrow we will be in another parade. Just marching around the drill grounds.

Why don't you write to me? I haven't heard from you yet. I suppose it's in the mail though. I have noticed that it sometimes takes four or five days for mail to reach me.

You had better cash these checks soon because they are quite old.

Please put them right on my account with the other money.

Love Buddy.

January 13, 1944

Dear Mom,

I got a letter from Hazel and one from Jean yesterday and a box of candy from Pop today.

I have two checks enclosed that I want you to put in the bank for me.

We may get off for 36 hours instead of 12 on our first liberty. This will be if we are the cleanest company. Both yesterday and today we were the cleanest. I sure ~~her we~~ hope we win because then I could come home for a day.

I think I told you that we were on dish-washing detail for two days. We are all through with that now. We took two more shots this afternoon, one in each arm.

I just got through washing my clothes. The whites that I was wearing when I was doing the dishes were pretty muddy. I scrubbed on them for about a half an hour, but they still were tattle tale gray.

Tomorrow we will be in another parade. Just marching around the drill grounds.

Why don't you write to me? I haven't heard from you yet. I suppose it's in the mail though.

I have noticed that it sometimes takes four or five days for mail to reach me.

You had better cash these checks soon because they are quite old. Please put them right on my account with the other money.

Love,

Buddy

# Chapter Four

# A Short History of the *USS WASP*

## Part I

## Design and Construction

Following World War I, the United States, Great Britain, France, Italy, and Japan signed the *Washington Naval Treaty* in 1922 that limited the tonnage of various types of warships, and the total tonnage of all warships. This was affirmed in 1932 with some modifications that included submarines and destroyers. In 1936, with world tensions increasing, Japan and Italy left the agreement and it subsequently collapsed.

With the collapse of the *Treaty*, the Navy was free to design new, larger class of aircraft carrier utilizing lessons learned from the earlier construction of the *Yorktown* class. The resulting "*Essex* class" of aircraft carriers were longer, wider, included deck elevators, enhanced anti-aircraft armament, and increased aircraft capacity. Using that improved design, the *USS Oriskany* was commissioned and started construction in March of 1942, at the Bethlehem Shipbuilding's Fore River Shipyard in Quincy, Massachusetts.

In the fall of 1942, the *USS Oriskany*'s name was changed to the *USS WASP* honoring an aircraft carrier of the same name (CV-7) that had been recently torpedoed by a Japanese submarine and then scuttled in the South Pacific. With World War II raging, the Bethlehem Shipbuilding Corporation was pushed to finish the carrier. The *USS WASP* (CV-18) was launched on August 17, 1943. It entered commission on November 24, 1943, with Captain Clifton A. F. "Ziggy" Sprague in command.

**Captain Clifton Sprague**

## Preparing for Combat

Following a shakedown cruise and then alterations in the shipyard, the *USS WASP* (CV-18) conducted training exercises in the Caribbean Sea before departing for the Pacific on January 10, 1944. Arriving at Pearl Harbor on April 4, the carrier continued training and subsequently sailed for Majuro, the capital of the newly-captured Marshall Islands where it joined Vice Admiral Marc "Pete" Mitscher's "Fast Carrier" Task Force 58.

**Vice Admiral Marc Mitscher**

## *USS WASP* (CV18) Specifications:

- Displacement: 27,100 tons
- Length: 872 ft.
- Beam: 93 ft.
- Draft: 34 ft., 2 in.
- Propulsion: 8 boilers, 4 Westinghouse steam turbines, 4 shafts
- Speed: 33 knots
- Complement: 2,600 men

## Armament:

- 4 twin five-inch .38 caliber guns
- 4 single five-inch .38 caliber guns
- 8 × quadruple 40 mm .56 caliber guns
- 46 × single 20 mm .78 caliber guns
- 90-100 aircraft

**USS WASP in February of 1944**

# Chapter Five

## Waiting for Advanced Training

As is common in all branches of the military, the slogan is "hurry up and wait!" Bud is now done with Basic Training and is waiting for the Navy to assign him a school so he can proceed with his Advanced Individual Training (AIT). He does not know what he will be doing and the Navy does not seem interested in telling him as this point. In World War II, soldiers and sailors served at the convenience of their branch of the military and were not given a choice of their MOS (Military Occupation or Service). People enlisted in the Navy because they felt it was a better option than service with the Army or the Marines (there was no Air Force during World War II as each branch had its own aviation branch, *i.e.*, Army Air Corps).

Bud also tells us about his recent experience going on "sick call." At the opening formation (reporting for duty), A man who reports sick is excused to go to the infirmary where a medical corpsman would assess his problem (called Triage). In Bud's case, since he had an infection, they immediately put him in the hospital. They kept him there for three or four days before they returned him to his unit.

Holdover duty is never fun. It is those times in your military career when you are waiting to go to your next duty station. In Bud's case, he got more KP duty washing dishes. He worked very long hours and did not get paid any overtime. Called "details," practically any job can be a thankless one, but they have to be done. The Navy feeds a lot of people three times a day, which means there are lots of dishes to be washed.

Bud is also trying to sell his car and his bike but not having much success. Cars became an albatross during the War because gas was rationed and getting more than eight gallons a week required a lot of paperwork. Even if you finished the paperwork, it was greeted by hostile bureaucrats.

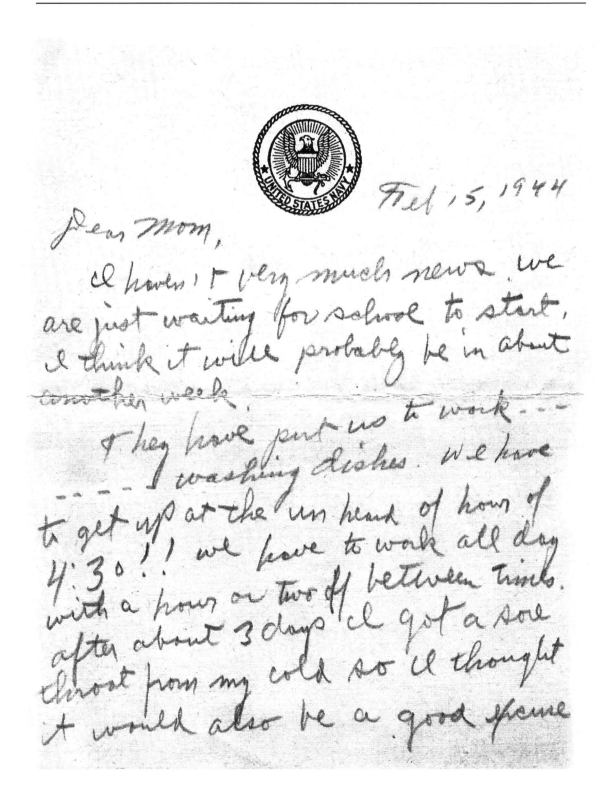

Feb 15, 1944

Dear Mom,

I haven't very much news. We are just waiting for school to start. I think it will probably be in about another week.

They have put us to work --- --- washing dishes. We have to get up at the un heard of hour of 4:30!! we have to work all day with a hour or two off between times. after about 3 days I got a sore throat from my cold so I thought it would also be a good space

to get sick. U had a tempture so
they put me to bed in the hospital.
U was there for 3 or 4 days and
caught up on all my sleep. the first
time U have been fully awake for about
a month. U got out this afternoon
but U have to start back to work
tomorrow.

U don't know when U will get to
come home. U hope before school
starts.

from Buddy.

p. s. Uf you any body who wants
to buy a car or a bike sell them.

February 15, 1944

Dear Mom,

I haven't very much news. We are just waiting for school to start. I think it will probably be in about another week.

They have put us to work... washing dishes. We have to get up at the unheard hour of 4:30!!! We have to work all day with a hour or two off between times.

After about three days I got a sore throat from my cold so I thought I would also be a good excuse to get sick. I had a temperature so they put me to bed in the hospital. I was there for three or four days and caught up on all my sleep, the first time I have been fully awake for about a month. I got out this afternoon, but I have to start back to work tomorrow.

I don't know when I will get to come home. I hope before school starts.

Love,

Buddy


P. S. If you have anybody who wants to buy a car or a bike, sell them.

# Chapter Six

## Car and Bike for Sale

As one might expect, Bud is now writing his father to get his car sold, something his father is probably not pleased about having to do. Most servicemen ended up having their family put their car up on jacks in a garage somewhere so they can use it again without wearing out the tires (we forget that tires in those days lasted only ten to fifteen thousand miles).

During the War, gas was rationed, so people could only get gas if they had stamps allowing them to buy it... no stamps, no gas. Bud did what a lot of sailors and soldiers did, they gave their ration book to their family in the hope they could use them before they expired.

Even though this letter is written just two days after the previous one, it is written to his father, not his mother.

He also bemoans the fact that he will not get home before his advanced training starts. He tries to put it in the best light possible.

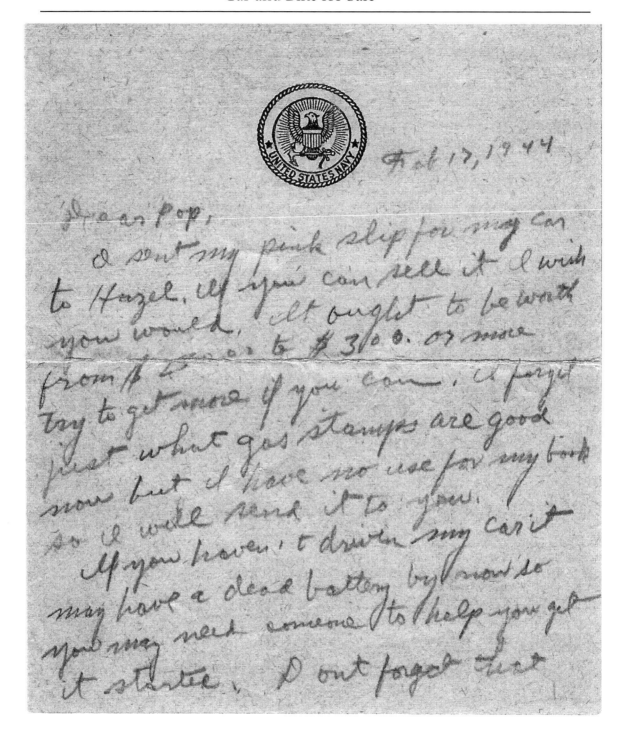

Feb 17, 1944

Dear Pop,

I sent my pink slip for my car to Hazel. If you can sell it I wish you would. It ought to be worth from $ _____ to $300.00 or more. Try to get more if you can. I forgot just what gas stamps are good now but I have no use for my book so I will send it to you.

If you haven't driven my car it may have a dead battery by now so you may need someone to help you get it started. Don't forget that the door on the left side does not work and on the right side it works only from inside, so <u>don't close the door when the window is up</u>. If you can sell the bike go ahead and do that too. get as much as you can for that.

My school will start in another week or more but I am not sure. I don't know if I will get to come home before then or not.

You eat too much but I think I eat more now because of the stuff we are eating.

February 17, 1944

Dear Pop,

I sent my pink slip for my car to Hazel. If you can sell it, I wish you would. It ought to be worth from $250-$300 or more. Try to get more if you can. I forget just what gas stamps are good now but I have no use for my book so I will send it to you.

If you haven't driven my car, it may have a dead battery by now so you may need someone to help you get it started. Don't forget that the door on the left side does not work and on the right side it works only from the inside so don't close the door when the window is up.

**Gas Ration Stamps from the War**

If you can sell the bike go ahead and do that too. Get as much as you can for that.

My school will start in another week or more, but I am not sure. I don't know if I will get to come home before then or not.

You fart too much but I think I fart more now because of the stuff we are eating.


No salutation or signature

# Chapter Seven

## Liberty This Weekend!

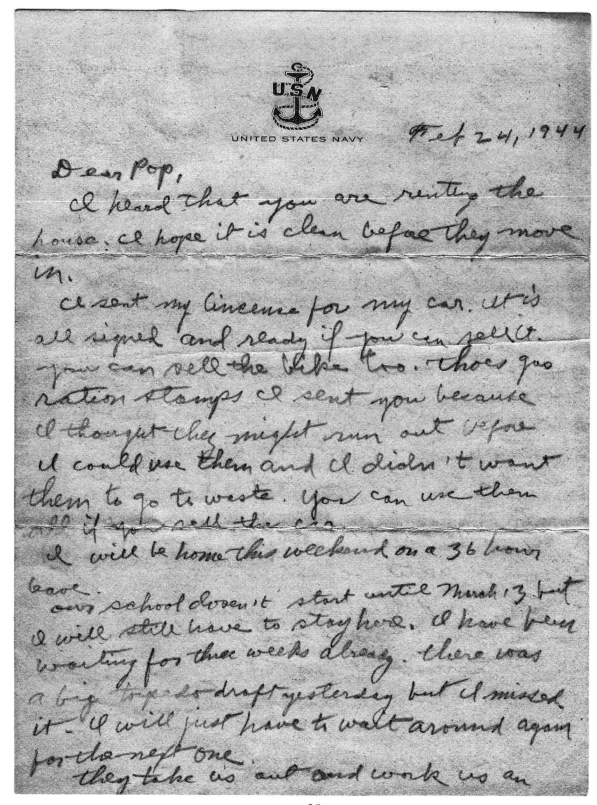

UNITED STATES NAVY

Feb 24, 1944

Dear Pop,

I heard that you are renting the house. I hope it is clean before they move in.

I sent my lincense for my car. It's all signed and ready if you can sell it. You can sell the bike too. Those gas ration stamps I sent you because I thought they might run out before I could use them and I didn't want them to go to waste. You can use them all if you sell the car.

I will be home this weekend on a 36 hour leave. Our school doesn't start until March 13 but I will still have to stay here. I have been waiting for three weeks already. There was a big torpedo draft yesterday but I missed it. I will just have to wait around again for the next one.

They take us out and work us an

hour or so a day to keep us busy but the rest of the time we just loaf around. They could just as easily let us go home but the Navy and I don't agree.

The first three weeks they had us on a dishwashing job so that's why I couldn't get home. But now we get a 36 hour liberty every other weekend.

In boot camp our mail was delivered to us, but now we have to go after it ourselves.

Are they still making hell for you by making you work at the other plant on Sunday? Did you ever get a sleeping bag?

Well I don't have very much news now or until school starts.

Hazel said that you wanted me to write some letters to you but the reason I write most of them to her is because that is more or less the center of information and if I write only to there the news will get around just as fast. But why don't you write to me?

While I had the dish washing job I had to get up with the chickens or even before them at 4:30 but now since I have been relieved of that job I get up at 6:00. it is much better.

I never saw much of San Diego but once last week when I was on liberty I went to the Good Humor plant here, He was just about to leave to make a road so I went along. We went for quite a ride

I wrote to Milt Smith at Good Humor (Hollywood) and got him to arrange a load to S. D. when I come so I will get a free ride back in the big truck. Well I can't think of much more to say so I will see you over the weekend.

so long you old fart,

Buddy

P. S. you fart too much, you fart too much, you fart to much. - - - - I am sending this letter to Hazel because you might not get it at the House.

February 24, 1944

Dear Pop,

I heard that you are renting the house. I hope it is clean before the move-in.

I sent my license for my car. It is all signed and ready. If you can sell it you can sell the bike too. Those gas ration stamps I sent you because I thought they might run out before I could use them, and I didn't want them to go to waste. You can use them all if you sell the car.

I will be home this weekend on a 36-hour leave. Our school doesn't start until March 13 but I will still have to stay here. I have been waiting for three weeks already.

There was a big torpedo draft yesterday but I missed it. I will just have to wait around again for the next one. They take us out and work us an hour or so a day to keep us busy but the rest of the time we just loaf around. They could let us go home but the Navy and I don't agree.

The first three weeks they had us on a dish washing job so that is why I couldn't get home but now we got a 36-hour liberty every other weekend.

In boot camp our mail was delivered to us but now we have to go after it ourselves.

Are they still making hell for you by making you work at the other plant on Sunday? Did you ever get a sleeping bag?

Well I don't have very much news now or until school starts. Hazel said that you wanted me to write some letters to you but the reason I write most of them to her is because that is more or less the center of information and if I write only to her the news will get around just as fast. But why don't you write to me? While I had the dish-washing job I had to get up with the chickens or even before them at 4:30 but now since I have been relieved of that job I get up at 6 o'clock. It is much better I never saw much of San Diego but once last week when I was on liberty I went to the Good Humor plant here. He was just about to leave to make a road call out where some truck broke down so I went along. We went for quite a ride.

I wrote to Milt Smith at Good Humor (Hollywood) and got him to arrange a load to San Diego when I come so I will get a free ride back in the big truck.

Well, I can't think of much more to say so I will see you over the weekend.

So long you old fart.

Buddy

P. S. You fart too much. You fart too much. You fart too much. I am sending this letter to Hazel because you might not get it at the house.

# Chapter Eight

# Rationing

## The War Affects the Home Front

Soon after the Japanese attack on Pearl Harbor and America's subsequent entry into World War II, it became apparent to government officials that voluntary conservation on the home front was not going to suffice. Restrictions were placed on imported foods, limitations were placed on the transportation of goods due to a shortage of rubber tires, and a diversion of agricultural harvests to soldiers overseas all contributed to the U.S. government's decision to ration certain essential items. On January 30, 1942, the Emergency Price Control Act was passed granting the Office of Price Administration (OPA) the authority to set price limits and ration food and other commodities in order to discourage hoarding and ensure the equitable distribution of scarce resources. By the spring, Americans were unable to purchase sugar without government-issued food coupons. Vouchers for coffee were introduced in November, and by March of 1943, meat, cheese, fats, canned fish, canned milk, and other processed foods were added to the list of rationed provisions.

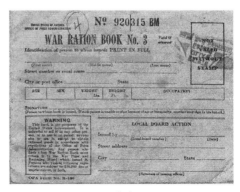

Ration Book from 1943

To get a classification and rationing stamps, one had to appear before a local War Price and Rationing Board which reported to the OPA. Each person in a household received a ration book, including babies and small children who qualified for canned milk not available to others.

To receive a gasoline ration card, individuals had to certify their need for gasoline and prove to the Board that they owned of no more than five tires. All tires in excess of five per driver were confiscated by the government, because of rubber shortages.

An "A" sticker on a car was the lowest priority of gasoline rationing and entitled the car owner to three to four U.S. gallons of gasoline per week. "B" stickers were issued to workers in the military industry, entitling their holder of up to eight U.S. gallons of gasoline per week. "C" stickers allowed their users to obtain unlimited fuel. The "C" sticker was granted to persons deemed "very essential to the war effort," such as physicians and executives in the "War" Industry. There were other stickers too; M, T, and X, for special vehicles and needs.

A national "Victory Speed Limit" of 35 miles per hour was imposed to save fuel and rubber for tires in May of 1942.

# Chapter Nine

## Nobody's Home

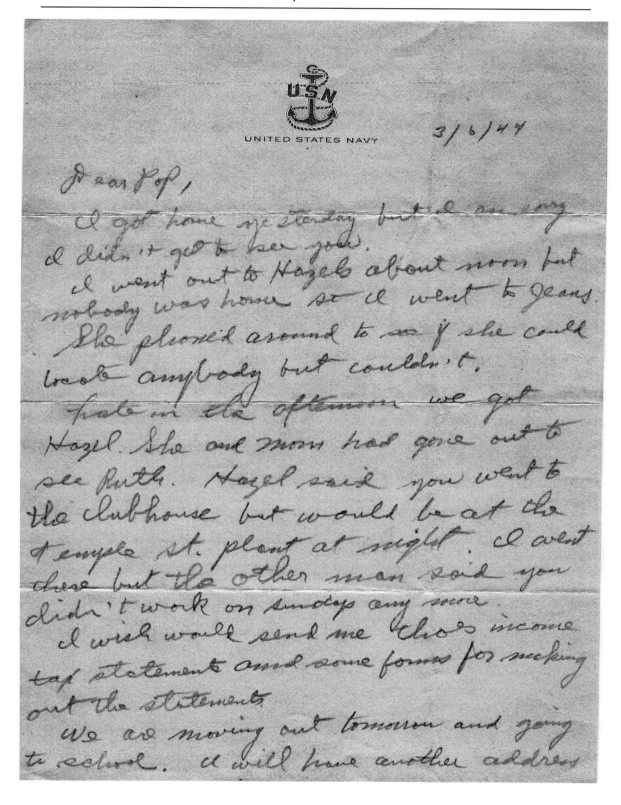

UNITED STATES NAVY

3/6/44

Dear Pop,

I got home yesterday but I am sorry
I didn't get to see you.

I went out to Hazels about noon but
nobody was home so I went to Jeans.
She phoned around to see if she could
locate anybody but couldn't.

Late in the afternoon we got
Hazel. She and mom had gone out to
see Ruth. Hazel said you went to
the clubhouse but would be at the
temple st. plant at night. I went
there but the other man said you
didn't work on sundays any more.

I wish would send me Theo's income
tax statements and some forms for making
out the statements.

We are moving out tomorrow and going
to school. I will have another address

then but you can use this one now until I get my new ones.

As I was [?] [?] in the other day I saw my car in the garage at Potters. What are they doing to it and what will it cost?

Please get the forms for making out the tax statements and those statements for how much money I made as soon as possible because the deadline is just one more week.

March 6, 1944

Dear Pop,

I got home yesterday but I am sorry I didn't get to see you. I went out to Hazel's about noon but nobody was home so I went to Jean's. She's phoned around to see if she could locate anybody but couldn't. Late in the afternoon we got Hazel. She and Mom had gone out to see Ruth. Hazel said you went to the clubhouse but would be at the Temple Street plant at night. I went there but the other man said you didn't work on Sundays anymore.

I wish you would send me those income tax statements and some forms for making out the statements.

We are moving out tomorrow and going to school. I will have another address then but you can use this one now until I get my new ones. As I was hitchhiking in the other day I saw my car in the garage at Potter's. What are they doing to it and what will it cost?

Please get the forms for making out the tax statement and those statements for how much money I've made as soon as possible because the deadline is just one more week .


not signed

# Chapter Ten

## Preparing for School

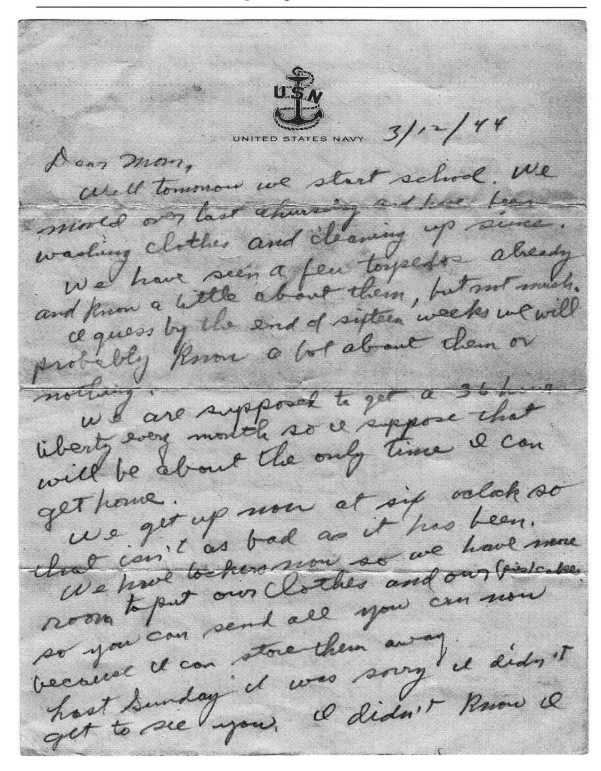

U.S.N

UNITED STATES NAVY      3/12/44

Dear Mom,

Well tomorrow we start school. We moved over last thursday and have been washing clothes and cleaning up since.

We have seen a few torpedos already and know a little about them, but not much. I guess by the end of sixteen weeks we will probably know a lot about them or nothing.

We are supposed to get a 36 hour liberty every month so I suppose that will be about the only time I can get home.

We get up now at six oclock so that isn't as bad as it has been.

We have lockers now so we have more room to put our clothes and our (fruitcake) so you can send all you can now because I can store them away.

Last Sunday I was sorry I didn't get to see you. I didn't know I

was going to get off until the last
minute so nobody knew I was comming.
I went to Hazels but nobody was
home so I went to Jeans.

At night when I was ready to come
back I went down to the bus depot
and was waiting in line to buy my
ticket, when a chief walked up and
said he had room for one more to
S.D. for $2.00. He had two other sailors
and a marine. I guess he made money
hauling them around. The bus fare was
$1.98 so I spent only 2 cents more
and got here quicker and had a seat
where I probably would have to stand
if I got on the bus.

In this class about half of them are
from a camp in Idaho. They say
it is so cold up there, they were all
wearing long underwear. It looked so funny.
By the way, my address here is:

P. Herwein S 2 C
18A torpedo school
group 2
U.S.N.T.S.
San Diego 33, Calif.    Love Buddy.

March 12, 1944

Dear Mom,

Well tomorrow we start school. We moved over last Thursday. Have been washing clothes and cleaning up since. We have seen a few torpedoes already and know a little about them, but not much. I guess by the end of 16 weeks we will probably know a lot about them or nothing.

We are supposed to get a 36-hour liberty every month so I suppose that will be about the only time I can get home.

We get up now at six o'clock so that isn't as bad as it has been. We have lockers now so we have some room to put our clothes and our pies and fruitcakes so you can send all you can now because I can store them away.

Last Sunday I was sorry I didn't get to see you. I didn't know I was going to get off until the last minute so nobody knew I was coming. I went to Hazel's but nobody was home so I went to Jean's. At night, when I was ready to come back, I went down to the bus depot and was waiting in line and a chief walked up and said he had room for one more to San Diego for two dollars. He had two other sailors and a marine. I guess he made money hauling them around. The bus fare was $1.98 so I spent only two cents more and I got here quicker and had a seat where I probably would have to stand if I got on the bus.

In this class about half of them are from a camp in Idaho. They say it is so cold up there. They were all wearing long underwear. It looked so funny.

By the way, my address here is

P. Heaverin S2c
18 Torpedo School, Group 2 USNTC
San Diego 33 California

Love,

Buddy

# Chapter Eleven

## The First Days of Torpedo School

UNITED STATES NAVY

march 14, 1944

Dear Mom,

well we started school finally. I'm still in the fog as far as a torpedo concerned but I think I'll catch on eventually.

We have two big tests coming up at the end of the week. I know just about all of one of them and part of the other one so I think I'll be okay.

I think I'll get a 36 hour liberty this weekend, probably the last for a while because we get only one a month from now on.

We have to write at least one letter each week home, so that's why I am writing now. I already wrote to you earlier this week but I already mailed it so it didn't count.

I think the food here is a little bit better than what we have been getting. But what we had was so bad that this isn't much better.

The last couple of nights it has been kind of rainy here and cold.

I got a letter from Don Woods

*yesterday. He is down in tops somewhere.*
*Well I had better get some studying done before I go to bed so I'll close now.*
*Love*
*Buddy*

March 14, 1944

Dear Mom,

Well, we started school finally. I'm still in the fog as far as a torpedo is concerned but I think I'll catch on eventually. We have two big tests coming up at the end of the week. I know just about all of one of them and part of the other one so, I think I'll be OK.

I think I get a 36-hour liberty this weekend, probably the last for a while because we get only one a month from now on.

We have to write at least one letter each week home so that's why I am writing now. I already wrote to you earlier this week, but I already mailed it, so it didn't count.

I think the food here is a little bit better than what we have been getting, but what we had was so bad that this isn't much better.

The last couple of nights it has been kind of rainy here and cold.

I got a letter from Don Woods yesterday. He is down in Texas somewhere.

Well, I had better get some studying done before I go to bed so I'll close now.

Love,

Buddy

15 MARCH – EN ROUTE TO PANAMA CANAL ZONE.

21 MARCH – PASSED THROUGH CANAL. STOPPED FOR A DAY AT BALBOA. CONTINUED ON TO SAN DIEGO TO PICK UP MAXIMUM PLANE LOAD AND PASSENGERS.

28 MARCH – MOORED AT NORTH ISLAND, SAN DIEGO.

30 MARCH – LEFT FOR PEARL HARBOR AFTER LOADING 100 EXTRA PLANES, 2,800 MARINES, LOADED ADDITIONAL CREW.

# Chapter Twelve

## Perrin "Bud" Burriss Heaverin, Jr.

## Biography - Part II

Buddy was off to war... Just as hundreds of thousands of young men (and now women), have done for centuries. He was adjusting to the shipboard routine and duties of the crew of the *USS WASP*.

The ship had recently joined the fleet at an advanced base to begin their career that included every major fleet action of World War II from then until the final days of the War. The *USS WASP* crews were awarded eight battle ribbons commemorating the combat action against the Japanese Navy. Buddy described one of his memorable occasions.

> It is a tradition that when one crosses the equator, one enters the realm of King Neptune, an initiation takes place. We "Polliwogs" run a gauntlet of "Shellbacks," armed with paddles who swatted us as we ran past them. We were then threatened having our teeth pulled by the "Dentist" wielding a pair of huge three feet long tongs. Finally, we were issued a certificate signed by King Neptune himself, making us full-fledged "Shellbacks" authorized to terrorize the next victims.

**Author's Note:** This age-old tradition is still practiced today, even on cruise ships and other vessels for passengers and crew crossing the equator for the first time.

Buddy was full of "sea stories." He wrote about some of them when he returned home.

> On one of our many trips into a primitive anchorage for re-supply, some of the crew were allowed to go ashore for a few hours of relaxation. These shore parties were provided with some sandwiches, a couple of cases of beer, a baseball, and a bat.

One young sailor (not me) had perhaps one beer too many, so he decided to take a nap under a coconut tree. When he awoke, the barge to the ship had left, and he watched helplessly as a ship steamed off over the horizon. He was later rescued by another beer party from another ship. He rejoined his ship by way of a bucket strung on a rope and pulled over a set of pulleys above the surging waves between the two ships. He was thereafter nicknamed Mog Mog, the name of the island where he was marooned.

Buddy couldn't tell his parents much about what was going on because all letters were censored. The following was written by Bud when he wrote his life story(so far) as requested by his sister, Hazel, 15-20 years later.

My duties were switchboard operator, mail censer, rocket fin assembler, gun loading crew, sweeper, and captain of the head (toilet). We rinsed our mops by trailing them over the side for several miles.

**The Mk-14 Torpedo as Shown by Submarine Officers
and Officials of the U.S. Navy Bureau of Ordinance**

# Chapter Thirteen

## On Board the *USS WASP*

Even though Bud never admits it to his family, he must have done well in his basic training and in Navy Torpedo School. The Navy assigned him to one of their new aircraft carriers: the *USS WASP*. He would spend the rest of the War on this ship. The rest of these letters tell the story of his life aboard the *USS WASP*.

To safeguard the secrecy in the event the mailbag fell into Japanese hands, the *USS WASP*'s crew couldn't reveal what was actually happening aboard ship. The ship's censors made sure of that! However, Naval Law requires that all ships maintain a log recording all their activities. This log always stays with the ship. Excerpts of this log are in this book. We will use an icon as a separator between Bud's letter and the ship's log. This icon is shown below:

As you continue to read, notice that the date on Buddy's letters are close to, or the same as the date of the entries in the ship's log. This ties the **Life** of Bud and the **Life** of the WASP together. Both want victory. Both want to survive.

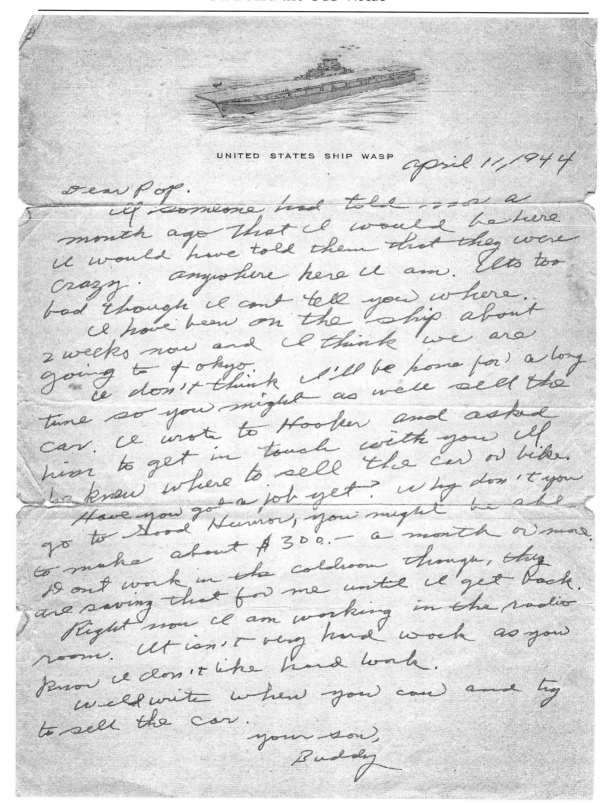

UNITED STATES SHIP WASP

april 11, 1944

Dear Pop,

If someone had told me a month ago that I would be here I would have told them that they were crazy. anywhere here I am. Its too bad though I can't tell you where.

I have been on the ship about 2 weeks now and I think we are going to Tokyo.

I don't think I'll be home for a long time so you might as well sell the car. I wrote to Hooker and asked him to get in touch with you. If he knew where to sell the car or bike.

Have you got a job yet? Why don't you go to Good Humor, you might be able to make about $300.— a month or more. I don't work in the coldroom though, they are saving that for me until I get back.

Right now I am working in the radio room. It isn't very hard work as you know I don't like hard work.

Well write when you can and try to sell the car.

your son,
Buddy

April 11, 1944

Dear Pop,

If someone had told me a month ago that I would be here I would have told them that they were crazy. Anyhow, here I am. It's too bad though I can't tell you where? I have been on the ship about two weeks now and I think we are going to Tokyo.

I don't think we will be home for a long time so you might as well sell the car. I wrote to Hooker and asked him to get in touch with you if he knew where to sell the car or bike.

Have you got a job yet? Why don't you go to Good Humor, you might be able to make about $300 a month or more? Don't work in the cold room though, they are saving that for me until I get back.

Right now, I am working in the radio room. It isn't very hard work, as you know I don't like hard work.

Well write when you can and try to sell the car.

Your son,

Buddy

11 APRIL – MOORED AT NAVY YARD, PEARL HARBOR.

Bud would later explain to his family:

> One morning across the bay a large aircraft carrier steamed in. The next thing I knew I was struggling up a steep gangplank, with my ninety-pound pack on my back. I was a member of the crew of the *USS WASP*. The next morning we were on our way to Hawaii with a crew of over 3,000 plus 5,000 servicemen/passengers. We also had extra airplanes. We were packed to the gills with people and equipment. We were escorted by two destroyers, one on each side.

# Chapter Fourteen

## Telephone Operator

april 11, 1944

Dear Mom,

Well I don't have a lot to say. We haven't been doing much. I went on liberty a few days ago and got some pictures taken. I haven't mailed them yet but I will.

I got a doll for Jeanette.

I haven't got any mail from home yet, I guess it will take time.

Last Sunday Easter was just the same as any other day. We hardly know one day from the next they all seem the same.

I got a new job for just while we are in port. I am a telephone operator. I started last night. The first time someone called I gave him the wrong number twice. I made a lot of mistakes for a while because a lot of calls would come at once and then it would be quiet for a while

Well I don't know very much more to say so I better close now. I hope I get some mail soon, please write!

Love,
Buddy

April 11, 1944

Dear Mom,

Well I don't have a lot to say. We haven't been doing much. I went on liberty a few days ago and got some pictures taken. I haven't mailed them yet but I will.

I got a doll for Jeanette. (his niece)

I haven't got any mail from home yet. I guess it will take time.

Last Sunday, Easter was just the same as any other day. We hardly know one day from the next. They all seem the same.

I got a new job for just while we are in port. I am a telephone operator. I started last night. The first time someone called I gave him the wrong number twice. I made a lot of mistakes for a while because a lot of calls would come at once and then it would be quiet for a while.

Well I don't know very much more to say so I better close now. I hope I get some mail soon. Please write.

Love,

Buddy

3 APRIL – MOORED AT FORD ISLAND, PEARL HARBOR, OAHU, T. H.[1]

7 APRIL – SORTIED FROM PEARL HARBOR FOR TWO DAY GUNNERY EXERCISES AND DAY AND NIGHT FLIGHT QUALIFICATIONS.

9 APRIL - MOORED AT FORD ISLAND, PEARL HARBOR.

**Author Note:** SORTIED means "movement of ship or planes from a defensive position for training exercises or to attack the enemy, then return.

[1]T.H. = Territory of Hawaii as Hawaii did not become a state until August 21, 1959.

# Chapter Fifteen

## The Official USS WASP Telephone Operator

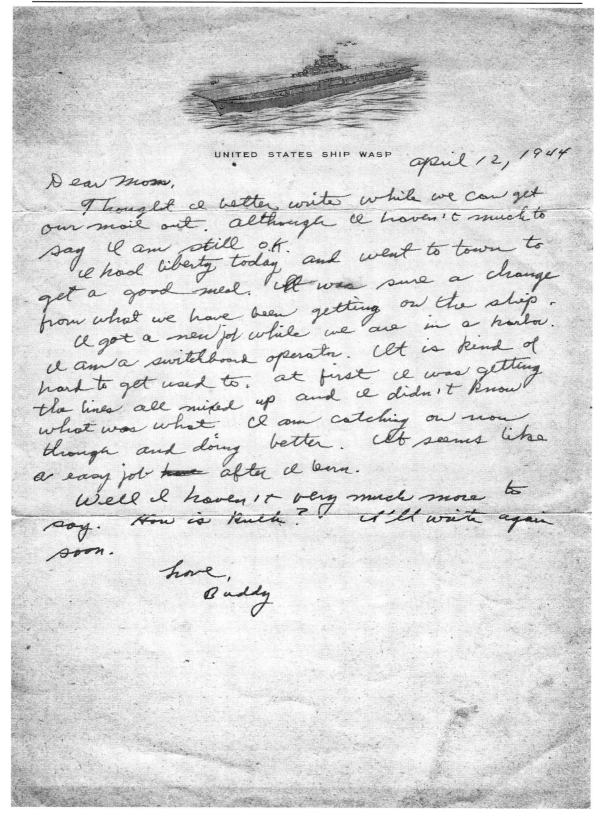

UNITED STATES SHIP WASP

April 12, 1944

Dear Mom,

Thought I better write while we can get our mail out. Although I haven't much to say I am still O.K.

I had liberty today and went to town to get a good meal. It was sure a change from what we have been getting on the ship.

I got a new job while we are in a harbor. I am a switchboard operator. It is kind of hard to get used to. At first I was getting the lines all mixed up and I didn't know what was what. I am catching on now though and doing better. It seems like a easy job after I learn.

Well I haven't very much more to say. How is Ruth? I'll write again soon.

love,
Buddy

April 12, 1944

Dear Mom,

I thought I better write while we can get our mail out although I haven't much to say. I am still OK.

I had liberty today and went to town to get a good meal. It was sure a change from what we have been getting on the ship.

I got a new job while we are in a harbor. I am a switchboard operator. It is kind of hard to get used to. At first I was getting the lines all mixed up and I didn't know what was what. I am catching on now though and doing better. it seems like an easy job after I learn.

Well I haven't very much more to say. How is Ruth? I'll write again soon.

Love,

Buddy

16 APRIL – SORTIED FROM PEARL HARBOR FOR TWO DAY GUNNERY EXERCISES, EXPERIMENTAL CATAPULTING OF P-47, AND AIR OPERATIONS.

18 APRIL – MOORED AT FORDS ISLAND, PEARL HARBOR. LOADED STORES.

# Chapter Sixteen

## News From Home

After the December 7, 1941, surprise attack by the Japanese and the devastating losses at Pearl Harbor, the future looked bad for the United States. On the one hand it was in the American spirit to "strike back". On the other hand, but with what? How? The U.S. needed to show some willingness to fight, to "get back up off the mat" and actively resist the enemy.

Within four months, on April 18, 1942, Doolittle's Raiders, a squadron of B-25 bombers made a surprise and successful raid on the Japanese capital: Tokyo. On August 7, 1942, we saw the invasion of Guadalcanal Island. This effectively slowed Japanese aggression in the Pacific. Yes, our country was on the way back!

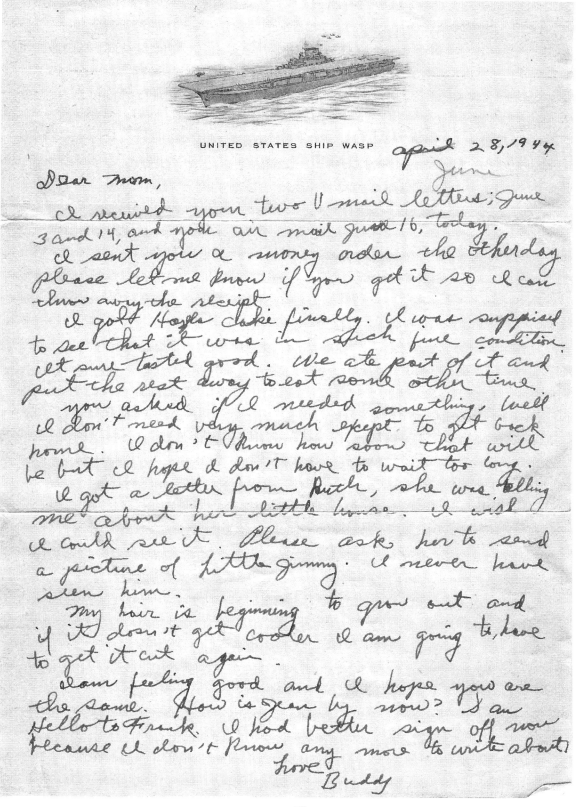

UNITED STATES SHIP WASP

April 28, 1944

Dear mom,

I received your two V mail letters; June
3 and 14, and your air mail June 16, today.

I sent you a money order the otherday
please let me know if you get it so I can
throw away the reciept

I got Hazels cake finally. I was surprised
to see that it was in such fine condition.
It sure tasted good. We ate part of it and
put the rest away to eat some other time.

You asked if I needed something, Well
I don't need very much except to get back
home. I don't know how soon that will
be but I hope I don't have to wait too long.

I got a letter from Ruth, she was telling
me about her little house. I wish
I could see it. Please ask her to send
a picture of little Jimmy. I never have
seen him.

My hair is beginning to grow out and
if it doesn't get cooler I am going to have
to get it cut again.

I am feeling good and I hope you are
the same. How is Jean by now? Say
Hello to Frank. I had better sign off now
because I don't know any more to write about.
love
Buddy

April 28, 1944

Dear Mom,

I received your two V mail letters, June 3 and 14 and your air mail June 16 today.

I sent you a money order the other day. Please let me know if you get it so I can throw away the receipt.

I got Hazel's cake finally. I was surprised to see that it was in such fine condition. We ate part of it and put the rest away to eat some other time.

You asked if I needed something. Well, I don't need very much except to get back home. I don't know how soon that will be but I hope I don't have to wait too long.

I got a letter from Ruth. She was telling me about her little house. I wish I could see it. Please ask her to send a picture of little Jimmy. I never have seen him.

My hair is beginning to grow out and if it doesn't get cooler I am going to have to get it cut again.

I am feeling good and I hope you are the same. How is Jean by now? Say hello to Frank. I had better sign off now because I don't know anymore to write about.

Love,

Buddy

21-23 APRIL – OPERATED OUT OF PEARL HARBOR CONDUCTING GUNNERY EXERCISES, AND REFRESHING AND QUALIFYING PILOTS OF DIFFERENT AIR GROUPS.

REMAINED MOORED UNTIL 3 MAY.

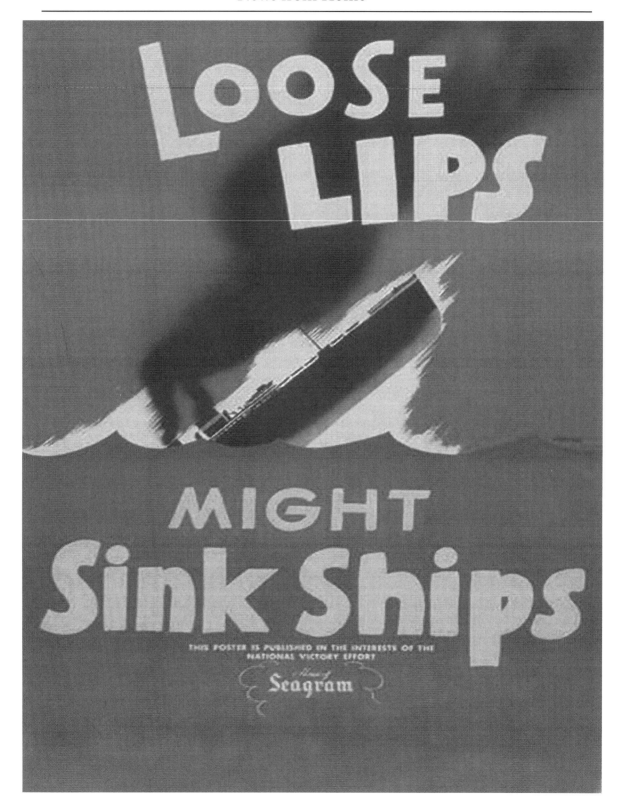

# Chapter Seventeen

## Packages

**Author Note:** While Buddy was away getting ready to fight the Japanese, the war news at home was very sobering. I read the *Baltimore Sun* newspaper every night. On the front page, outlined with a black border, was the list of Baltimore men killed and wounded received that day. Sometimes the lists were extensive, more than five to ten. This experience was common throughout the country. As I mentioned previously, the honored custom was to hang a small blue star flag in the window of the home representing a family member in the armed forces. If that family member had died in action, the star was gold.

May 1, 1944

Dear Mom,
    Just to let you know that I am still alright! Last week they started letting us send packages home so I bought a few things and they are in the mail now. I don't know whats wrong with my mail but I have only gotten your 2 letters so far, I should have had more by now but I haven't.
    We haven't been doing very much except have a lot of inspections the last few days.
    It sure is hot here. It seems like summer all the time. You said in your last letter that Ruth was going to move. Will you please send me your her new address as soon as possible.

            Love, Buddy

May 1, 1944

Dear Mom,

Just to let you know that I am still all right.

Last week they started letting us send packages home so I bought a few things and they are in the mail now. I don't know what's wrong with my mail but I have only gotten your two letters so far. I should have had more by now but I haven't.

We haven't been doing very much except have a lot of inspections the last few days.

It sure is hot here. It seems like summer all the time.

You said in your last letter that Ruth was going to move. Will you please send me her new address as soon as possible.

Love,

Buddy

MOORED AT FORD ISLAND, PEARL HARBOR.

**Author Note:** Concerning the foregoing letter to Mom, the censor cut out the picture of the ship and the caption identifying the ship???

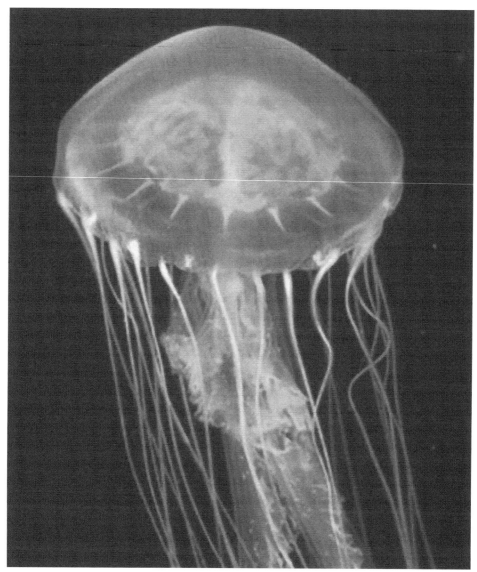

**Jellyfish**

# Chapter Eighteen

## Jellyfish

MAY 11, 1944

DEAR MOM,

I RECEIVED YOUR LETTER TODAY. AND WAS GLAD TO HEAR
FROM YOU. I ALSO GOT A LETTER FROM HOOKER. HE SAID THAT
HE HAD TAKEN ANOTHER ONE OF HIS TRIPS. TO EL PASO THIS
TIME. IT SEEMS THAT EACH TIME HE TAKES A TRIP HE GOES
FURTHER.

YESTERDAY THEY LET US GO SWIMING OVER THE SIDE. IT
WAS PRETTY GOOD BECAUSE IT HAS BEEN SO HOT. THE WATER IS
CLEAR BUT HAS A LOT OF JELLY FISH IN IT. IT LOOKS JUST
LIKE A WHITE MASS. IT ITCHES THE SKIN IF ANY GETS ON THOUGH
IT LOOKS LIKE A LOT OF XXXKXXX MOSQUITO BITES BUT IT DOSEN'T
LAST VERY LONG.

HOW IS EVERYTHING AT HOME? WHAT IS RUTH'S ADDRESS NOW?
THE CHOW IS EITHER GETTING BETTER OR ELSE I AM GETTING
USED TO IT. A FEW WEEKS BACK WE WERE ALOWED TO SEND BACK XXX
THE THINGS THAT WE BOUGHT. PLEASE LET ME KNOW WHEN YOU GET
THEM.

IT HAS BEEN SO HOT THAT WE ONLY WEAR OUR UNDERSHIRTS NOW.
IT RAINS ALMOST EVERY DAY AND SURE SEEMS DIFFERENT THAN CALIF.

WE HAVE BEEN TRAVELING SO MUCH THAT I WOULD LIKE TO KNOW
WHERE WE ARE SO CAN YOU GET ME A MAP SO I CAN HAVE SOME IDEA
WHERE WE ARE. WE              WELL I DON'T KNOW ANY
MORE TO WRITE ABOUT SO I BETTER SIGN OFF NOW.

LOVE,

Buddy

May 11, 1944

Dear Mom,

I received your letter today and was glad to hear from you. I also got a letter from Hooker. He said that he had taken another one of his trips to El Paso this time. It seems that each time he takes a trip he goes further.

Yesterday they let us go swimming over the side. It was pretty good because it has been so hot. The water is clear but has a lot of jellyfish in it. It looks just like a white mass. It itches the skin if any get on (you) though. It looks like a lot of mosquito bites but it doesn't last very long.

How is everything at home? What is Ruth's address now?

The chow is either getting better or else I am getting used to it.

A few weeks back we were allowed to send back the things that we bought. Please let me know when you get them.

It has been so hot that we only wear our undershirts now. It rains for almost every day and sure seems different than California. We have been traveling so much that I would like to know where we are so can you get me a map so I can have some idea where we are. We (CENSORED) Well, I don't know any more to write about so I better sign off now.

Love,

Buddy

3 MAY- UNDERWAY FOR PACIFIC FLEET SECRET ANCHORAGE AT MAJURO ATOLL, MARSHALL ISLANDS. CONDUCTED TRAINING EXERCISES EN ROUTE.

8-14 MAY – AT ANCHOR (AREA FORMERLY OCCUPIED BY JAPANESE)

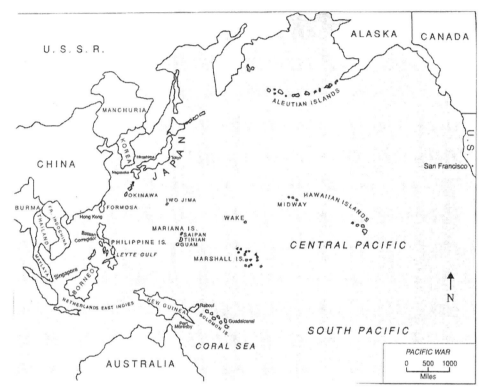

**Map Outlining the Pacific Theater of World War II**
**The *USS WASP* Traversed Much of This Area**

# Chapter Nineteen

## Indian Haircut

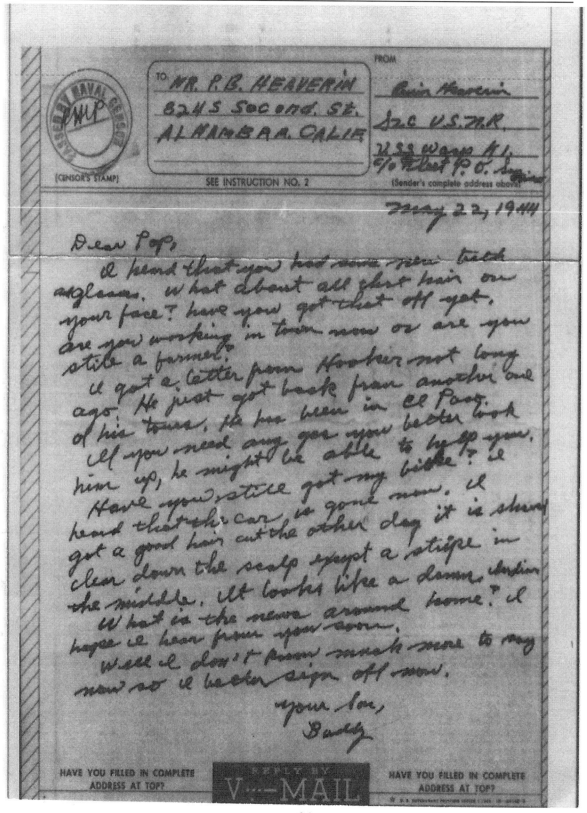

May 22, 1944

Dear Pop,

I heard that you had some new teeth and glasses. What about all that hair on your face? Have you got that off yet. Are you working in town now or are you still a farmer?

I got a letter from Hooker not long ago. He just got back from another one of his tours. He has been in El Paso. If you need any gas now better look him up, he might be able to help you.

Have you still got my bike? I heard that the car is gone now. I got a good hair cut the other day it is shaved clear down the scalp except a stripe in the middle. It looks like a damn Indian.

What is the news around home? I hope I hear from you soon.

Well I don't know much more to say now so I better sign off now.

your son,
Buddy

May 22, 1944

Dear Pop,

I heard that you had some new teeth and glasses. What about all that hair on your face? Have you got that off yet? Are you working in town now or are you still a farmer? I got a letter from Hooker not long ago. He just got back from another one of his tours. He has been in El Paso. If you need any gas you better look him up, he might be able to help you.

Have you still got my Bible? I heard the car is gone now. I got a good haircut the other day. It is shaved clear down to the scalp except a stripe in the middle. It looks like damn Indian.

What is the news around home? I hope I hear from you soon.

Well I don't know much more to say now so I better sign off now.

Your son,

Buddy

17 MAY RENDEZVOUSED WITH FUELING TASK UNIT.

19 MAY LAUNCHED FOUR STRIKES AGAINST MARCUS ISLAND

20 MAY LAUNCHED TWO STRIKES AGAINST MARCUS ISLAND. DESTROYED ENEMY AIRCRAFT, SURFACE CRAFT, AND SHORE INSTALLATIONS

# Chapter Twenty

## Still Board Ship

Notice Bud uses the words, "I am still alright" frequently. Perhaps it is to lessen the concerns of the family at home or his relief to be able to say that. He uses the term often after participating in dangerous situations, but he can't say any more than that because the censors would just strike it from his letters and he might get reprimanded by his officers.

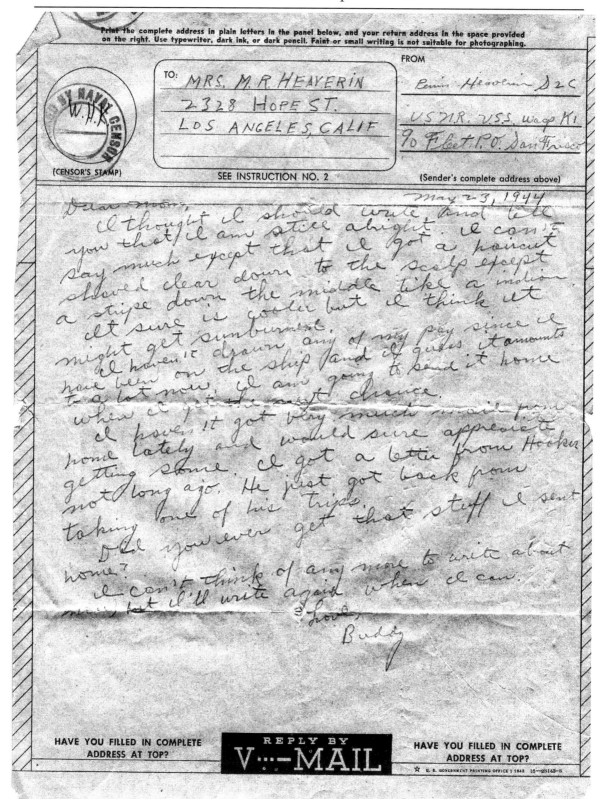

May 23, 1944

Dear Mom,

I thought I should write and tell you that I am still all right. I can't say much except that I got a haircut shaved clear down to the scalp except a stripe down the middle like a Indian. It sure is cooler but it might get sunburned.

I haven't drawn any of my pay since I have been on the ship and I guess it amounts to a lot now. I am going to send it home when I get the next chance.

I haven't got very much mail from home lately and I would sure appreciate getting some. I got a letter from Hooker not long ago. He just got back from taking one of his trips.

Did you ever get that stuff I sent home?

I can't think of any more to write about now but I'll write again when I can.

Love,

Buddy

23 MAY LAUNCHED FIVE STRIKES AGAINST WAKE ISLAND AIR, SURFACE, AND SHORE TARGETS.

**Author Note:** These strikes prevented Japanese forces from Wake Island from interfering with the impending assault of Saipan.

# Chapter Twenty-One

## Hazel's Cake

May 28, 1944

Dear Mom,

I got your letters dated May 4, 11, 15 yesterday and was glad to hear from you. I am glad that you got that package alright. I still haven't got Hazels cake yet. I hope it doesn't rot before I get it or I will have to feed it to the fishes.

If you don't get very much mail from me, it isn't because I don't want to write but because I don't have anything to say. I sure appreciate getting mail though and I usually keep my letters and read them several times.

I will be sending some money home soon. It isn't doing me any good here. You can either put it in the bank or buy some bonds with it.

I'll write again soon as I can.

Love,
Buddie

May 28, 1944

Dear Mom,

I got your letters dated May 4, 11, 15 yesterday and was glad to hear from you. I am glad that you got that package all right. I still haven't got Hazel's cake yet. I hope it doesn't rot before I get it or I will have to feed it to the fishes.

If you don't get very much mail from me, it isn't because I don't want to write but because I don't have anything to say. I sure appreciate getting mail though and I usually keep my letters and read them several times.

I will be sending some money home soon. It isn't doing me any good here. You can either put it in the bank or buy some bonds with it.

I'll write again soon as I can.

Love,

Buddy

28 MAY – CONTINUED LOADING SUPPLIES AS YESTERDAY.

Many years later, Buddy recalled some of his life aboard ship:

> The food was fair, lacking fresh fruit, or milk... names for most of them, unprintable (*e.g.*, SOS). We had a barter system going. If anyone had anything of value, it could be traded for extra food, our laundry ironed, first dibs on the ship's newspaper, a reserved seat at the movies, or jewelry made from used airplane parts. These people were called "BTOs" (big-time operators).

# Chapter Twenty-Two

## Am I Still Rich?

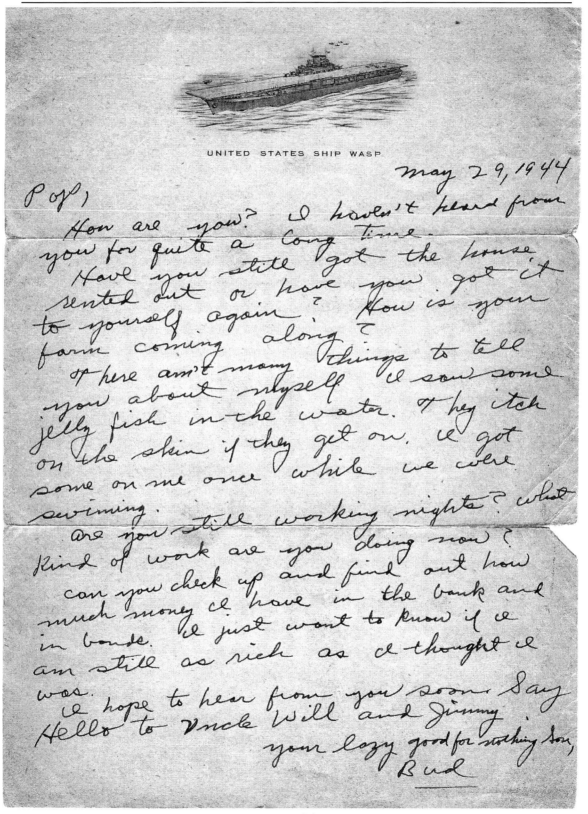

UNITED STATES SHIP WASP.

May 29, 1944

Pop,

How are you? I haven't heard from you for quite a long time.

Have you still got the house rented out or have you got it to yourself again? How is your farm coming along?

There ain't many things to tell you about myself. I saw some jelly fish in the water. They itch on the skin if they get on. I got some on me once while we were swimming.

Are you still working nights? What kind of work are you doing now?

Can you check up and find out how much money I have in the bank and in bonds. I just want to know if I am still as rich as I thought I was.

I hope to hear from you soon. Say hello to Uncle Will and Jimmy.

your lazy good for nothing son,
Bud

96

May 29, 1944

Dear Pop,

How are you? I haven't heard from you for quite a long time. Have you still got the house rented out or have you got it to yourself again? How is your farm coming along?

There aren't many things to tell you about myself. I saw some jellyfish in the water. They itch on the skin if they get on. I got some on me once while we were swimming.

Are you still working nights? What kind of work are you doing now?

Can you check up and find out how much money I have in the bank and IKN bonds? I just want to know if I am as still as rich as I thought I was.

I hope to hear from you soon. Say hello to Uncle Will and Jimmy.

Your lazy good-for-nothing son,

Bud

29 MAY – CONTINUED LOADING SUPPLIES.

# Chapter Twenty-Three

## The Practical Joke

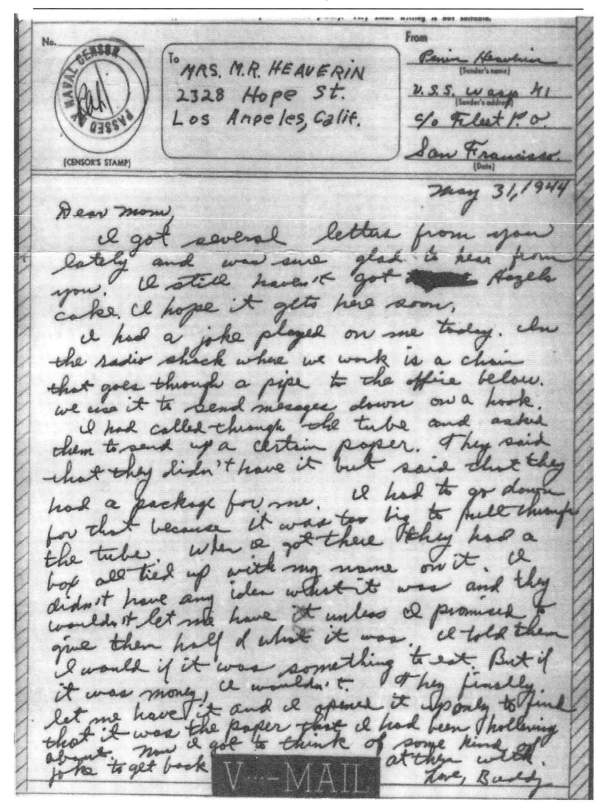

May 31, 1944

Dear Mom,

I got several letters from you lately and was sure glad to hear from you. I still haven't got Hazel's cake. I hope it gets here soon.

I had a joke played on me today. In the radio shack where we work is a chain that goes through a pipe to the office below. We use it to send messages down on a hook. I had called through the tube and asked they send up a certain paper. They said that they didn't have it but said that they had a package for me. I had to go down for that because it was too big to pull through the tube. When I got there they had a box of all tied up with my name on it. I didn't have any idea what it was and they wouldn't let me have it unless I promised to give them a half of what it was. I told them I would if it was something to eat but if it was money I wouldn't. They finally let me have it and I opened it up only to find what it was the paper that I had been hollering about.

Now I got to think of some kind of joke to get back at them with.

Love,

Buddy

31 MAY –MOORED AT MAJURO. (Marshall Islands)

**Hot and Wet**

# Chapter Twenty-Four

## Money and Rain

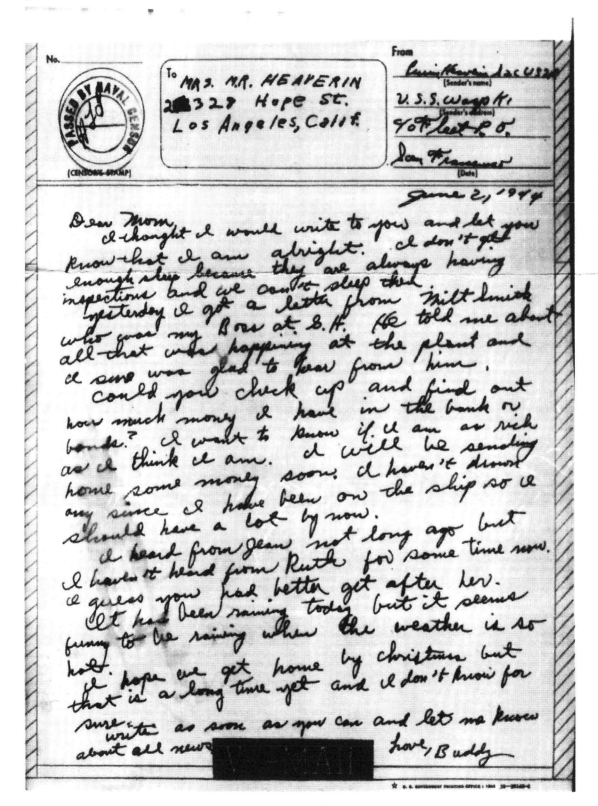

To MRS. M.R. HEAVERIN
2327 Hope St.
Los Angeles, Calif.

From
[Sender's name]
U.S.S. Wasp K,
90th Fleet P.O.
[Date]

June 2, 1944

Dear Mom,
I thought I would write to you and let you know that I am alright. I don't get enough sleep because they are always having inspections and we can't sleep then. Yesterday I got a letter from Milt Smith who was my Boss at S.H. He told me about all that was happening at the plant and I sure was glad to hear from him.

Could you check up and find out how much money I have in the bank or bonds? I want to know if I am as rich as I think I am. I will be sending home some money soon; I haven't drawn any since I have been on the ship so I should have a lot by now.

I heard from Jean not long ago but I haven't heard from Ruth for some time now. I guess you had better get after her.

It had been raining today but it seems funny to be raining when the weather is so hot. I hope we get home by christmas but that is a long time yet and I don't know for sure. Write as soon as you can and let me know about all news.

love, Buddy

June 2, 1944

Dear Mom,

I thought I would write to you and let you know that I am all right. I don't get enough sleep because they are always having inspections and we can't sleep then.

Yesterday I got a letter from Milt Smith who was my boss at Good Humor. He told me about all that was happening at the plant, and I sure was glad to hear from him. Could you check up and find out how much money I have in the bank or bonds? I want to know if I am as rich as I think I am. I will be sending home some money soon. I haven't drawn any since I have been on the ship so I should have a lot by now.

I heard from Jean not long ago, but I haven't heard from Ruth for some time now. I guess you had better get after her.

It has been raining today but it seems funny to be raining when the weather is so hot.

I hope we get home by Christmas but that is a long time yet and I don't know for sure.

Write as soon as you can and let me know about all news.

Love,

Buddy

2 JUNE – UNDERWAY OVERNIGHT TO CONDUCT GUNNERY TRAINING. RETURNED TO ANCHORAGE AT MAJURO.

# Chapter Twenty-Five

## Unkie Wants Some Japs

At this point in time, The *USS WASP* was seeing a lot of action. It was encouraging to the crew that those at home were trying to do their part. A young boy of 10 told a local paper about his effort to support the war effort.

> Saturdays, I scour my extended neighborhood to collect old newspapers. I have a regular route and people save papers and excess cooking fat and grease for me. I tie the papers in manageable bundles and load them in the family car. Mom drives me and my load to the Refuse Center. The Center pays me so much per hundred pounds. On a good day I get close to two dollars cash. I buy "War Savings Stamps" with my earnings.[1]

---

[1] During the War and thereafter, students were encouraged to buy war stamps once a week and paste them in a War Savings Stamp book to trade, when full, for a War Savings Bond. The stamps were in different denominations of ten cents, 25 cents, 50 cents, one dollar, and five dollars. A 25-cent stamp book, when full, represented $18.75, but when redeemed for a U.S. Savings Bond, Series E, it was worth $25 at maturity.

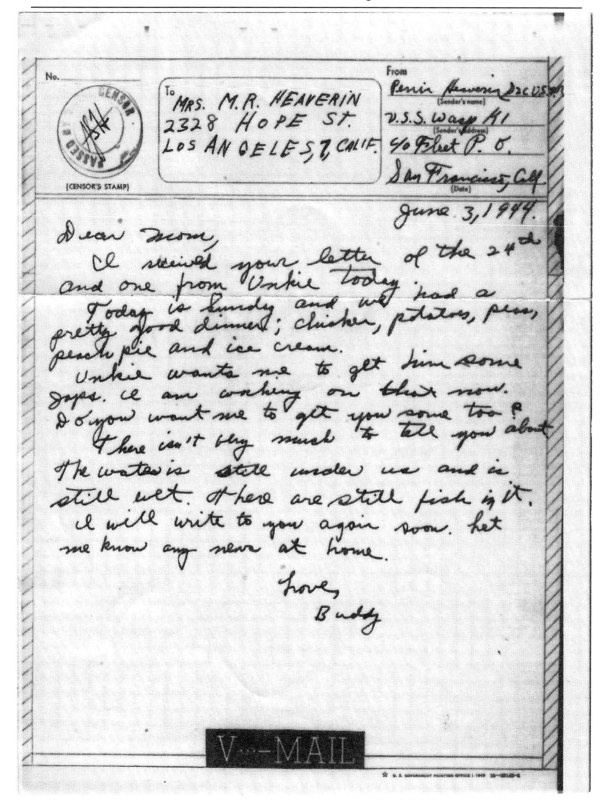

June 3, 1944

Dear Mom,

I received your letter of the 24th and one from Unkie today. Today is Sunday and we had a pretty good dinner: chicken, potatoes, peas, peach pie, and ice cream.

Unkie wants me to get him some Japs. I am working on that now. Do you want me to get you some too?

There isn't very much to tell you about. the water is still under us and is still wet. There are still fish in it.

I will write to you again soon. Let me know any news at home.

Love,

Buddy

No Letters Until July 22, but the letter author and the *USS WASP* were busy:

11 JUNE – LAUNCHED FIGHTER STRIKE ON TINIAN

12 JUNE – LAUNCHED 201 SORTIES ON TINIAN TOWN AND AIRFIELDS DROPPING 690 TONS OF BOMBS.

13 JUNE – LAUNCHED STRIKES AGAINST SAIPAN AIRFIELDS AND SHIPPING

15 JUNE – LAUNCHED STRIKES AGAINST ROTA

16 JUNE – AIR SUPPORT FOR TROOPS INVADING SAIPAN

18 JUNE – WASP PLANES ASSISTED IN SEARCH FOR ENEMY TASK FORCE. NO SIGHTINGS.

19 JUNE – START OF TWO-DAY BATTLE OF THE PHILIPPINE SEA. WASP STEAMED 100 MILES WEST OF OGF GUAM WITH OTHER TASK GROUPS TO MEET THE JAPANESE. WASP WAS ATTACKED BY 8 "JUDY" JAP PLANES AND SHOT FOUR DOWN. WASP RECEIVED SHRAPNEL FROM BOMB MISS ON STARBOARD QUARTER AND PORT BOW. FOUR MEN ON A QUAD 40MM MOUNT WERE WOUNDED AND ONE KILLED, THE FIRST KIA FOR THE USS WASP (CV18). WASP GUNNERS AFT SHOT DOWN THREE PLANES DIVING AT THE SHIP. LUCKILY, THE WASP HAD A NEAR MISS 50 FEET OF THE PORT BEAM. WASP AIRCRAFT DOWNED 12 JAPANESE PLANES.

ENEMY TASK FORCE WAS SIGHTED 270 MILES AWAY. WASP LAUNCHED LARGE STRIKES OF FIGHTERS, BOMBERS AND TORPEDO PLANES. BY DAY'S END, WASP LOST ONE FIGHTER, ELEVEN BOMBERS AND THREE TORPEDO PLANES, ALTHOUGH MANY WERE LOST AT SEA ON THE WAY BACK BECAUSE OF LACK OF FUEL. MANY OF THE CREW MEMBERS WERE RESCUED BY SEARCHING SHIPS.

THE JAPANESE TASK FORCE SUFFERED MANY LOSSES IN SHIPS AND HUNDREDS OF AIRCRAFT. U.S. PILOTS CALLED IT THE "MARIANAS TURKEY SHOOT." THE ENEMY FLEET WITHDREW FROM BATTLE AND EVADED FURTHER ACTION DESPITE EFFORTS OF SEARCH PLANES TO LOCATE THEM.

24 JUNE – LAUNCHED STRIKE ON RUNWAYS OF PAGAN ISLAND IN THE MARIANAS

25-26 JUNE – EN ROUTE TO ENIWETOK LAGOON CONDUCTING ROUTINE SEARCHES AND PATROLS.

27 JUNE – ANCHORED IN ENIWETOK LAGOON.

3 JULY – RENDEZVOUSED WITH FUEL TASK GROUP FOR REFUELING.

4 JULY – LAUNCHED STRIKES AGAINST IWO JIMA, AIRFIELDS AND SHIPPING

6 JULY – LAUNCHED STRIKES AGAINST OROTO AIRFIELD, GUAM.

8 JULY – LAUNCHED STRIKES AGAINST AHGANA TOWN, GUAM, AND NEARFBY AIRFIELDS.

10 JULY – LAUNCHED STRIKES AGAINST PITI TOWN, GUAM.

14 JULY – LAUNCHED RECORD-MAKING AIR GROUP 14 IN STRIKES AGAINST GUN POSITIONS WEST OF AGANA TOWN, GUAM

15 JULY – AIRCRAFT STRUCK ROTA AIRFIELD AT TATACHO POINT.

16 JULY – WASP AIRCRAFT ATTACKED GUAM BIVOUAC AREAS WITH ONE-TON DAISY CUTTER BOMBS DEVASTATINGLY EXPLODING JUST ABOVE THE GROUND.

18 JULY – LAUNCHED FOUR AIR STRIKES ON GUAM TARGETS, BUILDINGS, GUN POSITIONS AT ADCLIUP POINT, ASAN VILLAGE, PITI TOWN, CABRAS ISLAND.

19 JULY – LAUNCHED FOUR STRIKES ON GUAM GUN INSTALLATIONS AT AGANA AND ANANTOS POINT.

20 JULY – LAUNCHED FIVE STRIKES AGAINST GUAM, GUN EMPLACEMENTS ON THE RIDGE BEHIND AGANA TOWN.

21 JULY – "W" DAY FOR MARINES LANDING ON GUAM. WASP ASSISTED IN SUPPORT BY LAUNCHING SIX STRIKES AGAINST TARGETS DESIGNATED BY THE AIR COORDINATOR.

**Author Note:** This begins a series of air assaults on Rota and Guam to "soften up" Japanese defenses on those islands and then to provide close air support for the Marines landing on those islands on July 21.

Readers will notice there is a long time between this letter of June 3 and the next one. Why is that? The servicemen were certainly writing. They were required to write at least one letter a week, and many wrote a lot more than that. Hey, remember, there's a war going on! Rest assured that the Navy, in this case, understood how vital to victory was the morale of the officers and men in remote, hard-to-reach locations. Buddy wrote about beach parties, movies aboard ship, and other activities that are important to morale, just like quality of the food and mail.

Remember that getting the mail picked up or delivered isn't the easiest thing to do when you are at war, when ships are at sea, weeks at a time.

Mail delivery usually happened when the ship was anchored or moored in port. It also occurred ship to ship, such as mail being routed via a fuel tanker. Mail, movies, other important communications were sent between ships by a pulley system established across the open water during the fueling process.

It is evident from Buddy's letters that he craved communication from home. Up to date reading material was a valued item to ease the boredom of shipboard life. It is also evident that he understood the pain of separation from parents and loved ones. He constantly tells them he is all right, knowing that they are getting radio and newspaper reports that show pictures and headlines of the wartime battles that likely included the *USS WASP*.

The *USS WASP* was involved in all the major naval battles of the war in the Pacific. Buddy was doing his part to help morale at home. The reader must understand that there was no television, just newsreel reports in movie theaters and occasional radio reports from the front lines — hard to do aboard ship. Cell phones wouldn't be in common use for another fifty years. There was no way to keep contact except through the cherished pieces of mail.

# Chapter Twenty-Six

## Kind of Busy

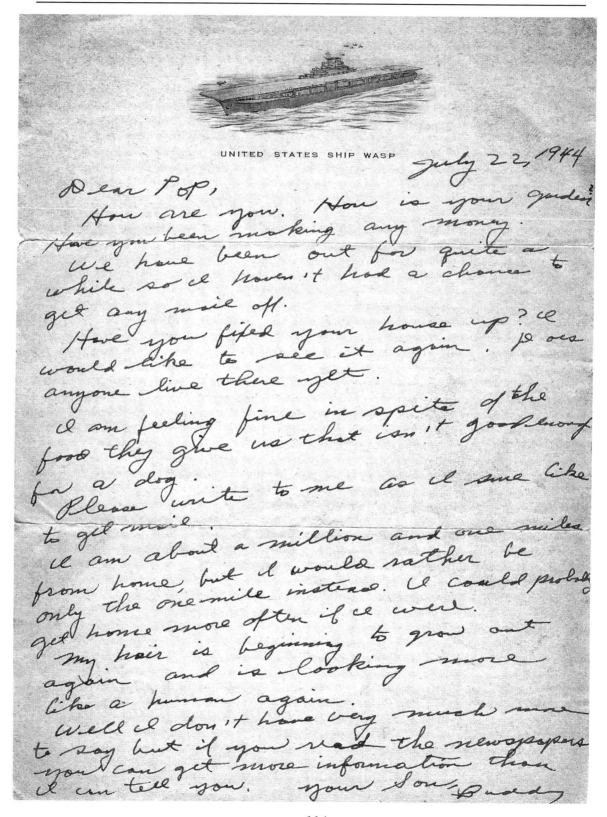

UNITED STATES SHIP WASP

July 22, 1944

Dear Pop,

How are you. How is your garden.
Have you been making any money.

We have been out for quite a
while so I haven't had a chance to
get any mail off.

Have you fixed your house up? I
would like to see it again. Does
anyone live there yet.

I am feeling fine in spite of the
food they give us that isn't good enough
for a dog.

Please write to me as I sure like
to get mail.

I am about a million and one miles
from home, but I would rather be
only the one-mile instead. I could probably
get home more often if I were.

My hair is beginning to grow out
again and is looking more
like a human again.

Well I don't have very much more
to say but if you read the newspapers
you can get more information than
I can tell you.    Your Son, Buddy

114

July 22, 1944

Dear Mom,

I am sorry that I haven't written you sooner but we were kind of busy so I couldn't. I got your letter June 16 not very long ago and haven't gotten any since.

I am feeling fine as ever and hope everyone at home is the same. Did you get the money order I sent not long ago? Let me know about it. I am sending my Social Security card so you can get the money if necessary.

How is everything at home? How is the weather by now? I haven't received any mail for a long time but expect some very soon. I'll write again after I get some and maybe by then I might have more to say.

Love,

Buddy

22 JULY – LAUNCHED BOMBING AND STRAFING STRIKES AGAINST GUAM GUN AND TROOP CONCENTRATIONS. DURING THE ENTIRE STRIKES AND NEUTRALIZATION OF GUAM, (Western Carolinas) ANTI-AIRCRAFT WAS MINIMAL AND AIRBORNE OPPOSITION WAS NIL.

23 JULY – UNDERWAY FOR AIR STRIKES OVER PALAU.

25 JULY – LAUNCHED STRIKES AGAINST PALAU ISLAND.

26 JULY – LAUNCHED STRIKES AGAINST THE USUAL BUILDINGS AND AIRCRAFT INSTALLATIONS, THIS TIME AGAINST KUROR ISLAND, BABELDAOB, ADAKNBOSON AND MALAKAL ISLANDS.

27 JULY – UNSCHEDULED STRIKES OVER KUROR TOWN, BABELDAOB FIELD AND MALAKAL ISLANDS.

# Chapter Twenty-Seven

## Million Miles From Home

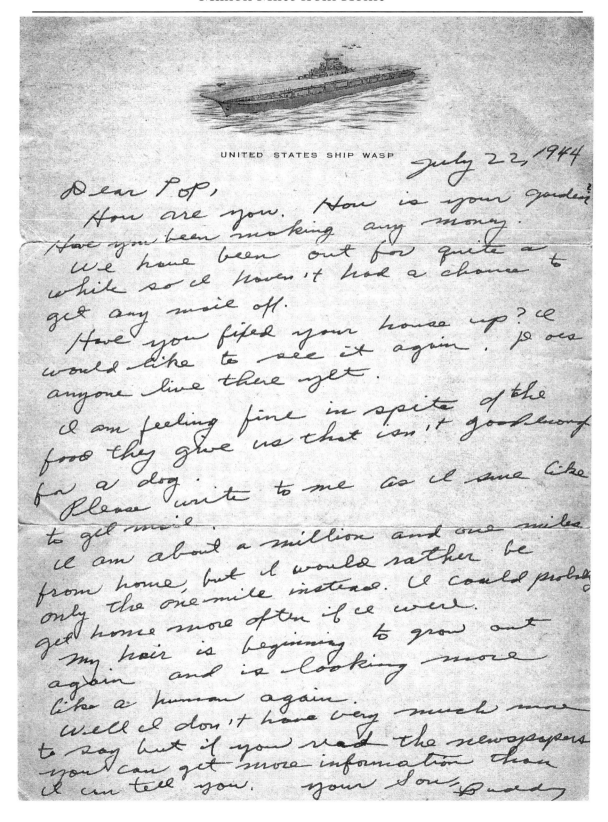

UNITED STATES SHIP WASP

July 22, 1944

Dear Pop,

How are you. How is your garden? Have you been making any money.

We have been out for quite a while so I haven't had a chance to get any mail off.

Have you fixed your house up? I would like to see it again. Does anyone live there yet.

I am feeling fine in spite of the food they give us that isn't good enough for a dog.

Please write to me as I sure like to get mail.

I am about a million and one miles from home, but I would rather be only the one-mile instead. I could probably get home more often if I were.

My hair is beginning to grow out again and is looking more like a human again.

Well I don't have very much more to say but if you read the newspapers you can get more information than I can tell you.

Your Son,
Buddy

118

July 22, 1944

Dear Pop,

How are you? How is your garden? Have you been making any money?

We have been out for quite a while so I haven't had a chance to get any mail off. Have you fixed your house up? I would like to see it again. Does anyone live there yet? I am feeling fine in spite of the food they give us that isn't good enough for a dog.

Please write to me as I sure like to get mail. I am about a million and one miles from home but I would rather be only one mile instead. I could probably get home more often if I were.

My hair is beginning to grow out again and is looking more like a human again.

Well I don't have very much more to say but if you read the newspapers you can get more information than I can tell you.


Your son,

Buddy

***************************************************

Buddy shared, in his after-war recollections:

I was in love with a photograph of a pretty sister of one of my shipmates. I asked my friend for her address. I wrote to her and she wrote back! We exchanged a few letters back and forth but nothing ever developed. So much for shipboard romance.

Life can be mighty lonely after long periods away from home, especially for a young man of 18 who has never been more than 100 miles from home.

Imaged by Heritage Auctions, HA.com

# Chapter Twenty-Eight

## Pretty Busy

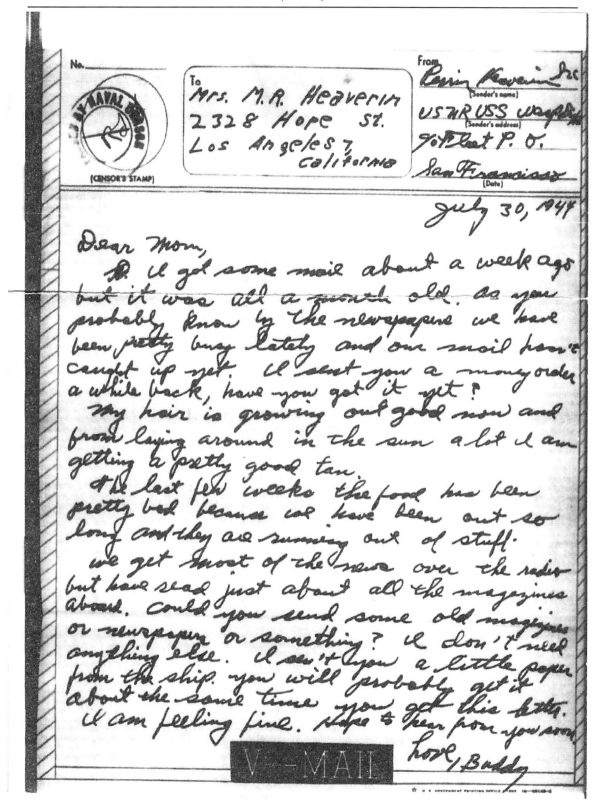

July 30, 1944

Dear Mom,

I got some mail about a week ago but it was all a month old. As you probably know by the newspapers we have been pretty busy lately and our mail hasn't caught up yet.

I sent you a money order a while back. Have you got it yet? My hair is growing out good now and from laying around in the sun a lot I am getting a pretty good tan.

The last few weeks the food has been pretty bad because we have been out so long and they are running out of stuff.

We get most of the news over the radio but I have read just about all the magazines aboard. Could you send some old magazines or newspapers or something. I don't need anything else.

I sent you a little paper from the ship. You will probably get it about the same time you get this letter. I am feeling fine hope to hear from you soon.


Your son,

Buddy

# Chapter Twenty-Nine

## Setting the Clocks Ahead

August 1, 1944

Dear Mom,

I got your letters, July 3, + 8, yesterday. Hope to get some more recent mail soon. I am feeling fine and hope everyone is well at home. Ruth sent Jim's address so I wrote to him the other day.

I sent you a little newspaper from the ship, have you got it yet?

I will send another money order soon. glad to hear you got it.

The food is pretty bad lately it is usually dehidrated or canned. There isn't anything I need for you to send except some magazines or newspapers.

My hair is almost grown out again and I am getting tan from laying around in the sun.

I will send some more pictures and things if we go back to Hawaii, but I expect that won't be soon.

Well its about time for chow. They set the clocks ahead another hour last night so we lost a hour sleep. They seem to be always changing the time of day.

Love Buddy

August 1, 1944

Dear Mom,

I got your letters, July 3 and 8 yesterday. Hope to get some more recent mail soon. I am feeling fine and hope everyone is well at home.

Ruth sent Jim's address so I wrote to him the other day. I sent you a little newspaper from the ship, have you got it yet? I will send another money order soon. Glad to hear you got it. The food is pretty bad. Lately, it is dehydrated or canned. There isn't anything I need for you to send except some magazines or newspapers.

My hair is almost grown out again and I am getting tan from laying around in the sun. I will send you some more pictures and things if we go back to Hawaii but I expect that won't be soon.

Well, it's about time for chow. They set the clocks ahead another hour last night so we lost a hour sleep. They seem to be always changing the time of day.[1]

Love,

Buddy

1 AUGUST – EN ROUTE TO ENIWETOK LAGOON.

---

[1]We have added Chapter 30 to explain Buddy's frustrations with time on board ship.

**Bud's Father's Poultry Market Where Bud Worked.
His Father is to the Left, Wearing a Suit as He Always Did.**

# Chapter Thirty

## Time Management in World War II

### Learning About Military Time

Draftees and recruits would learn very early in their training about the **Military Time** used in every branch of the United States Armed Forces. They would find out that our military uses a 24-hour time format that eliminates the need for "A.M." and "P.M." designations. The big reason the military institutions of the world adopted this system was because it left little or no room for confusion. Military Time is favored not only in the military community, but also in the scientific, medical, aviation, Information Technology (IT) and transportation communities. Many countries have adopted Military Time as their standard measurement of time including the United Kingdom (Great Britain), Germany, Australia, Canada, India, and the Philippines Republic.

To give an example of how Military Time works, 12:00 A.M. is referred to as either 2400 (twenty-four hundred) or 0000 hours. Clocks and computers displaying Military Time use 0000. 12:01 A.M. or 0001 hours is pronounced "zero-zero-zero-one." 5:23 A.M. or 0523 hours is spoken as "Zero five twenty-three." 11:41 a.m. or 1141 hours is spoken as "eleven forty-one." For P.M. times, one merely adds 1200 to the P.M. time to get Military Time. For example, 4:13 P.M. becomes 1613 hours (4:13 + 12:00) and is pronounced as "sixteen thirteen." 10:05 p.m. or 2205 hours (10:05 + 12:00) is spoken as "twenty-two zero five."

## MILITARY TIME CONVERSION CHART

| MILITARY TIME | REGULAR TIME | MILITARY TIME | REGULAR TIME |
|---|---|---|---|
| 0100 | 1:00 AM | 1300 | 1:00 PM |
| 0200 | 2:00 AM | 1400 | 2:00 PM |
| 0300 | 3:00 AM | 1500 | 3:00 PM |
| 0400 | 4:00 AM | 1600 | 4:00 PM |
| 0500 | 5:00 AM | 1700 | 5:00 PM |
| 0600 | 6:00 AM | 1800 | 6:00 PM |
| 0700 | 7:00 AM | 1900 | 7:00 PM |
| 0800 | 8:00 AM | 2000 | 8:00 PM |
| 0900 | 9:00 AM | 2100 | 9:00 PM |
| 1000 | 10:00 AM | 2200 | 10:00 PM |
| 1100 | 11:00 AM | 2300 | 11:00 PM |
| 1200 | NOON | 0000 or 2400 | MIDNIGHT |

## Military Dates

Many of these draftees and recruits also learn that the military has its own method of writing down dates on their reports and logs. The proper military date format includes the day, month and year, in that order. The format can be expressed as DD/MMM/YY with no commas. This indicates that:

- the day should have exactly two numbers so the first nine days of each month have a leading zero in front of the actual number.

- the month should have exactly three letters. That means that all months except for May must be abbreviated. Each abbreviation simply uses the first three letters of the month's name and  must be written in all capital letters.

- the year should have exactly two numbers. In those days, there was no risk of a century change, so two numbers was sufficient.

As a result, the military date format for the 3rd of July in 1944 would be written as 03 JUL 44. The months are written down as follows: January-JAN, February-FEB, March-MAR, April-APR, May-MAY, June-JUN, July-JUL, August-AUG, September-SEP, October-OCT, November-NOV, and December-DEC. When we came to the year 2000, many people wonders how years would be written. 1999 would be written as 99 while 2003 would be written as 03. In the computing world, they had to add two more places so computers could continue to calculate days.

## International designations

Sometimes, when Military Time is used, a letter is utilized to tell us what world time zone the time measurement is coming from. All time zones are measured from Greenwich Mean Time (from an observatory in Greenwich, England, United Kingdom). The world is divided into 24 time zones, each designated with a different letter of the alphabet as shown in the accompanying chart. To help identify the location of the time zone, a major city of the zone is shown. For example, 1545G means it is fifteen forty-five hours Golf, somewhere in the time zone that includes Bangkok, Thailand. It is also designated as Universal Time Coordinated (UTC) showing the difference in hours (+/-) from GMT.

## Military Time Zones Chart

| | | | |
|---|---|---|---|
| Alpha UTC +1 | Paris, France | November UTC -1 | Praia, Cabo Verde |
| Bravo UTC +2 | Munich, Germany | Oscar UTC -2 | Nuuk, Greenland |
| Charlie UTC +3 | Moscow, Russia | Papa UTC -3 | Sao Paula, Brazil |
| Delta UTC +4 | Dubai, UAE | Quebec UTC -4 | Halifox, Nova Scotia |
| Echo UTC +5 | New Delhi, India | Romeo UTC -5 | New York, NY |
| Foxtrot UTC +6 | Dhaka, Bangladesh | Sierra UTC -6 | Kansas City, MO |
| Golf UTC +7 | Bangkok, Thailand | Tango UTC -7 | Denver, CO |
| Hotel UTC +8 | Hong Kong, China | Uniform UTC -8 | Los Angeles, CA |
| India UTC +9 | Seoul, South Korea | Victor, UTC -9 | Juneau, AK |
| Kilo UTC +10 | Melbourne, Australia | Whiskey UTC -10 | Honolulu, HI |
| Lima UTC +11 | Honiara, Solomon Is. | X-Ray UTC -11 | Nome, AK |
| Mike UTC +12 | Auckland, New Zealand | Yankee UTC -12 | Suva, Figi Islands |
| Zulu UTC +0, Greenwich, United Kingdom (Great Britain) | | | |

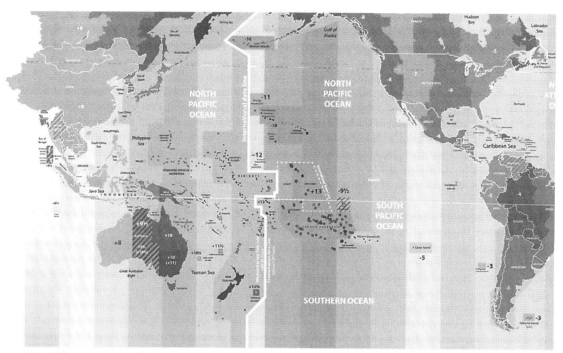

**World map: Vertical stripes depict the 24 time zones. Note white International Date Line.**

The *USS WASP* covered much of the Pacific Ocean and traversed time zones constantly. For that reason, the captain adjusted the ship's time, if necessary, at Midnight. That way, sailors like Buddy did not get confused about what time it was. Sailors also paid close attention to announcements over the intercom when it came to time.

# Chapter Thirty-One

## Checking Up on Dad

August 3, 1944

Dear Pop,

I hear you are getting your home all fixed up. How about writing and telling me all about it. Have you still got time to work your farm and your other job too? You must be busy.

How is your car, still going good? I haven't seen you since you got your teeth. Please send a picture of yourself and if you don't mind cut off that bush on your lip.

I guess you have been reading the papers as usual, please write and ask me some questions.

What are you going to do with that sign "Tom Turkies for sale 25 ¢lb." Is Nobol still in jail?

How is the gas ration book if you need any gas go see Hooker.

If Uncle Will is still saving the funnie papers, please send them to me as I sure would appreciate them.

It is still pretty hot and it rains often. I am getting a tan from being in the sun so much. My hair is growing back.

Well please write when you get a chance and if you don't have time write anyway.

your good for nothing son,
Bud

August 3, 1944

Dear Pop,

I hear you are getting your house all fixed up. How about writing and telling me about it. Have you still got time to work your farm and your other job too? You must be busy. How is your car, still going good? I haven't seen you since you got your teeth. Please send a picture of yourself and if you don't mind, cut off that bush on your lip.

I guess you have been reading the papers as usual. Please write and ask me some questions.

What are you going to do with that sign, "Tom Turkeys for sale $.25 a pound?"

Is Nobol still in jail? How is the gas ration book? If you need any gas go see Hooker.

If Uncle Will is still saving the funny papers, please send them to me as I sure would appreciate them.

It is still pretty hot and it rains often. I am getting a tan being in the sun so much. My hair is growing back.

Well please write when you get a chance and if you don't have time write anyway.

Your good for nothing son,


Bud

2 AUGUST — ANCHORED IN ENIWETOK LAGOON, PROVISIONED THE SHIP AND RESTED THE CREW UNTIL 29 AUGUST.

**The Sailors Getting a Little Time Off the Ship to Enjoy the Beach**

# Chapter Thirty-Two

## On the Beach

august 7, 1944

Dear Pop,

I got your letter today and I sure was glad to hear from you.

Hope you are settled in your house now. I sure wish I could see it. I bet it looks swell.

As you know we have been busy as hell the last couple of months. I wish I could tell you about it but you probably know as much as I from the newspapers.

Yesterday for the first time in over three months I was on solid ground. I took off my shoes and walked on the sand, rocks, and coconuts.

There was a very narrow beach with very pink sand. About fifty feet from the shore coconut trees were growing. It looked very much like pictures you've probably seen.

After going for a swim sombody started chasing each other in with all of their clothes on. Soon we were all wet so we stayed in clothes, shoes and all just to keep warm because there was quite a rain. (even in august). We all had a good time and returned to the ship safely.

Since we got back in port we have been getting pretty good food again. For

a while, at sea, it was beginning to
be pretty bad. They had run out of
a lot of things, except dehidrated spuds
that taste like ~~flour~~ flour. The
milk what we had of it was all canned
and tasted funny. We are eating better
now however. My hair is growing
back fine and I have a tan like
a central ave. nigger. I sweat most
of the time even when it rains. I
had my bedding out in the sun today
to get it aired and when I went
~~tho~~ to get it, it was raining and
was all wet

        I was looking at some of my
shoes the other day and found mold
growing them. I just crushed them
off and started wearing them putting
my other pair away. The next day I
looked again and found mold had
grown on them just over night. That
gives you a idea how hot it is here.
        Well I am just about out of news.
We have movies every night when we are
in port. Tonight we had one with
Eddie Cantor, sure was good.
        They only let us draw $10.- each
pay-day so it is stacking up, not
as fast as it used to though when
I was out, Ha.
        Well say hello to Uncle Will and
Jimmy Gormley. Hope to see you again
soon.    Your worthless Son,
                Bud

August 7, 1944

Dear Pop,

I got your letter today and I sure was glad to hear from you. Hope you are settled in your house now. I sure wish I could see it. I bet it looks swell.

As you know we have been pretty busy as hell the last couple of months. I wish I could tell you about it but you probably know as much as I from the newspapers.

Yesterday for the first time in over three months I was on solid ground. I took off my shoes and walked on the sand, rocks, and coconuts. There was a very narrow beach with very pink sand. About 50 feet from the shore coconut trees were growing. It looked very much like pictures you've probably seen. After going for a swim somebody started dunking each other in with all their clothes on. Soon we were all wet so we stayed in (the water) clothes, shoes and all just to keep warm because there was quite a rain (even in August). We all had a good time and returned to the ship safely.

Since we got back in port, we have been getting pretty good food again. For a while at sea, it was beginning to be pretty bad. They had run out of a lot of things except dehydrated spuds that taste like flour. The milk, what we had of it, was all canned and tasted funny. We are eating better now however. My hair is growing back fine and I have a tan like a Central Avenue nigger. I sweat most of the time even when it rains. I had my bedding out in the sun today to get it aired and when I went to get it, it was raining and all wet.

I was looking at some of my shoes the other day and found mold growing in them. I just brushed them off and started wearing them putting my other pair away. The next day I looked again and found mold had grown on them just overnight. That gives you an idea how hot it is here.

Well I am just about out of news. We have movies every night when we are in port. Tonight we had one with Eddie Cantor, sure was good.

They only let us draw $10 each payday so it is stacking up. Not as fast as it used to when I was out. Ha!

Well, say hello to Uncle Will and Jimmy Gormley. Hope to see you again soon.

Your worthless son,

Bud

ANCHORED IN ENIWETOK LAGOON UNTIL 29 AUGUST

**This is likely the movie Buddy saw.**

# Chapter Thirty-Three

## Still Keeping Busy

August 14, 1944

Dear Mom,

I haven't gotten any mail for three days now so I thought I had better write home and tell you how I am. I am still feeling fine and keeping busy. I hope you are alright by now.

I think I already mentioned that I got to go ashore the other day. We had a pretty good time although there wasn't any town just coconut trees and sand. The water was swell for swimming.

I haven't gotten any more packages in the mail except the cake that Hazel sent a while back.

It was too bad that the big old tree on ninth street fell down. It must have been a pretty big storm.

Is Jean back from her vacation yet? She must have had a pretty good time.

I got a letter the other day from Good Humor Co. They wanted me to write them a letter so I did.

Did you ever get that little paper I sent from the ship?

I'll write again soon.

Love Buddy

August 14, 1944

Dear Mom,

I haven't gotten any mail for three days now so I thought I had better write home and tell you how I am. I am still feeling fine and keeping busy. I hope you are all right by now. I think I already mentioned that I got to go I ashore the other day. We had a pretty good time although there wasn't any town, just coconut trees and sand. The water was swell for swimming.

I haven't gotten any more packages in the mail except the cake that Hazel sent a while back.

It was too bad that the big old tree on Ninth Street fell down. It must've been a pretty big storm.

Is Jean back from her vacation yet? She must have had a pretty good time.

I got a letter the other day from Good Humor Co. They wanted me to write them a letter so I did. Did you ever get that little paper I sent from the ship?

I'll write again soon.

Love,

Buddy

**Maybe the Most Famous Poster from World War II,**
**Interesting Sponsor Considering How Much Liquor They Sold to Soldiers and Sailors!**

# Chapter Thirty-Four

## The Beach Party

AUGUST 18, 1944

DEAR MOM,

I GOT YOUR PACKAGE TODAY AT LAST, IT WAS KIND OF GOOEY BUT TASTED SWELL. I DON'T KNOW WHAT IT LOOKED LIKE WHEN IT LEFT YOU BUT WHEN I GOT IT, IT WAS ALL RUN TOGETHER AND WAS VERY STICKY BUT IT SURE TASTED SWELL. YOU DIDN'T HAVE TO SEND THE SOAP AND TOOTH PASTE THOUGH, AS WE CAN BUY ALL THAT KIND OF STUFF ON THE SHIP, AND IT MAKES MORE POSTAGE THAT YOU HAD TO PAY FOR. IT WAS NICE OF YOU TO THINK OF IT ANYWAY THOUGH.

WE HAVE BEEN HAVING SOME PRETTY GOOD MOVIES LATELY WE HAVE BEEN IN FOR A WHILE NOW AND WE DIDN'T GET ANY WHILE WE WERE AT SEA FOR SO LONG.

THE MAIL HAS BEEN VERY SLOW AND NOT VERY MUCH OF IT. THE LATEST DATED LETTER I GOT SO FAR WAS AUG 4. I HOPE IT CATCHES UP WITH US SOON.

I MENTTONED BEFORE THAT WE GOT TO GO ASHORE FOR A BEACH PARTY WE HAD A SWELL TIME AND I THINK WE WILL GET TO GO AGAIN IN A DAY OR TWO. I GUESS I OUGHT TO HAVE SOME MORE NEWS BY THEN SO I BETTER CLOSE NOW. I AM FEELING FINE AND HOPE YOU ARE THE SAME. SAY HELLO TO EVERYONE.

LOVE,

Buddy

Being Heavin

August 18, 1944

Dear Mom,

I got your package today at last. It was kind of gooey but tasted swell. I don't know what it looked like when it left but when I got it... it was all run together and was very sticky but it sure tasted swell. You didn't have to send the soap and toothpaste though as we can buy all that kind of stuff on the ship and it makes more postage that you had to pay for. It was nice of you to think of it anyway though. We have been having some pretty good movies lately. We have been in (port) for a while now and we didn't get any while we were at sea for so long.

The mail has been very slow and not very much of it. The latest dated letter I got so far was August 4. I hope it catches up with us soon.

I mentioned before that we got to go ashore for a beach party. We had a swell time and I think we will get to go again in a day or two. I guess I ought to have some more news by then so I better close now.

I am feeling fine and hope you are the same. Say hello to everyone.

Love,

Buddy

## 18 AUGUST - STILL RESTING CREW

**Author Note:** The reader may notice the name Perry Heaverin written at the bottom of the page. Starting with this letter, readers will notice a check-mark is made on the letter when the censor officer had not only reviewed the letter for classified information but also noted that the writer had met the letter requirement (one per week).

On the Home Front, Car Pooling was Encouraged to Save Gasoline for the War Effort

# Chapter Thirty-Five

## Care Packages from Home

Aug 26, 1944

Dear Mom,

I got your V-mail letter yesterday and was very glad to hear from you. I got both your package and Hazels last week so I had quite a lot to eat. They were in pretty good condition but your candy was a little gooy.

We got to go on another beach party again yesterday. We had a swell time.

They took a picture of our division the other day so I'll send one home as soon as we get them.

There don't seem to be very much news to tell you. The mail isn't very fast getting here.

I don't know very much more to talk about. I am feeling fine.

Love
Buddy

P.S. I got your letter of Aug 17

Pvine Harvin

August 26, 1944

Dear Mom,

I got your V-mail letter yesterday and was very glad to hear from you. I got both your package and Hazel's last week so I had quite a lot to eat. They were in pretty good condition but your candy was a little gooey.

We got to go on another beach party again yesterday. We had a swell time.

They took a picture of our division the other day so I'll send one home as soon as we get them.

There doesn't seem to be very much news to tell you. The mail isn't very fast getting here. I don't know very much more to talk about. I am feeling fine.

Love,

Buddy

P. S.  I got your letter of August 17

21 AUGUST – UNDERWAY CONDUCTING ROUTINE FLIGHT OPERATIONS AND GUNNERY EXERCISES.

23 AUGUST – ANCHORED AT ENIWETOK LAGOON. PROVISIONING SHIP.

23 AUGUST – UNDERWAY FOR AIR STRIKES OVER PALAU

25 AUGUST – LAUNCHED STRIKES PALAU ISLAND

26 AUGUST – LAUNCHED STRIKES AGAINST BUILDINGS AND AIRCRAFT INSTALLATIONS ON KEROR ISLAND, BABELTHUAP, ARAKABESAN, AND MALAKAL ISLANDS.

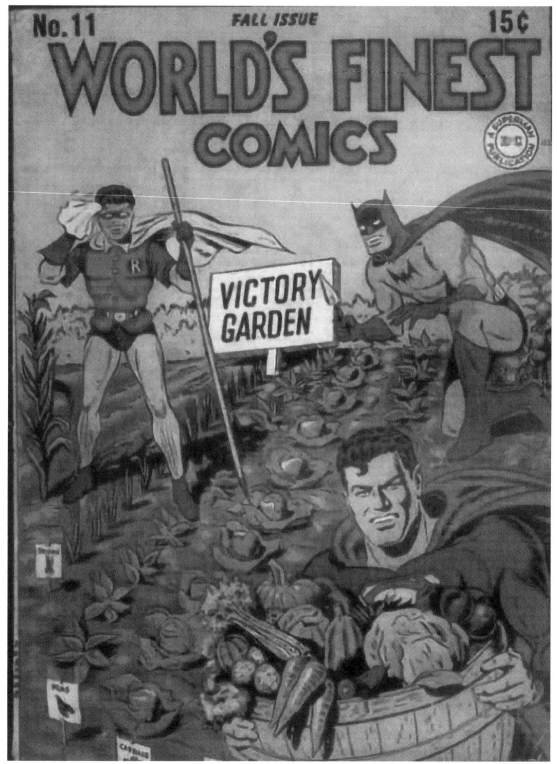

**Even the DC Comic Book Heroes Superman, Batman, and Robin
Were Employed to Bolster the Victory Garden Effort!**

# Chapter Thirty-Six

## Victory Gardens and Gophers

Aug 27, 194-

Dear Pop,

Well it is a nice Sunday morning so I decided I ought to write to you. I went to church this morning and just before that I wrote a letter to Hazel. I got your letter a while back and am just getting around to answering it. You must really think I am busy, but it is mostly laziness although I am very busy at times too.

Has anybody moved in your house yet? Hazel said that somebody was asking about it.

You must be kind of busy now with your garden along with your other job. Are you having anymore trouble with gophers this year? Did that cat ever come back or do you have to catch them all in traps.

We got to go ashore again the other day. The water was swell for swimming but that was about all there was to do, no town or nothing.

I don't suppose I will write very many letters for a while now because it will be a long time to get them off But don't worry.

How is uncle Will? Let me know about any news around town. Please write often so I'll get a big stack of mail. Well I better close now. I'll be thinking of you.  Your son,
Perin Heaven          Buddy

156

August 27, 1944

Dear Pop,

Well, It is a nice Sunday morning so I decided I ought to write to you. I went to church this morning and just before that I wrote a letter to Hazel. I got your letter a while back and I am just getting around to answering it. You must really think I am busy but it is mostly laziness, although I am very busy at times too.

Has anybody moved in your house yet? Hazel said that somebody was asking about it.

You must be kind of busy now with your garden along with your other job. Are you having any more trouble with gophers this year? Did that cat ever come back or do you have to catch them all in traps?

We got to go ashore again the other day. The water was swell for swimming but that was about all there was to do, no town or nothing.

I don't suppose I will write very many letters for a while now because it will be a long time to get them off (mailed) but don't worry. How is Uncle Will? Let me know about any news around town. Please write often so I'll get a big stack of mail.

Well, I better close now. I'll be thinking of you.

Your son,

Buddy

27 AUGUST LAUNCHED STRIKES OVER KEROR TOWN, BABELTHUAP FIELD, AND MALAKAL ISLAND

28 AUGUST – PREPARING TO GET UNDERWAY.

# The Victory Garden

During World War I, the famous agricultural scientist George Washington Carver wrote a tract in 1917 promoting the concept of a "Victory Garden." He saw it as a way for dealing with potential food shortages which he thought might happen if World War I lasted more than a couple of years. The tract outlined ways for people to begin growing vegetable gardens to help relieve pressures on the United States food supply. Shortly thereafter, the famous lumber magnate Charles Lathrop Pack organized the National War Garden Commission to promote the campaign.

Dr. George Washington Carver

When the United States was plunged into World War II with the Japanese attack on Pearl Harbor, the U.S. Department of Agriculture again encouraged the planting of "Victory Gardens" to relieve strains on the food supply. Even First Lady Eleanor Roosevelt planted a Victory Garden on the White House grounds, though she never tended it herself. The Department of Agriculture in tandem with large agribusiness organizations like International Harvester and Beech-Nut produced a massive number of booklets promoting both the Victory Garden concept and giving advice on practical gardening. By 1944, the fruits and vegetables harvested from Victory Gardens equaled commercial production of fresh vegetables.

After the War, the concept of Victory Gardens persisted around the United States, Most notably, the Dowling Community Garden in Minneapolis, Minnesota, where they continue to plant and raise vegetables.

# Chapter Thirty-Seven

## Return to Sea

Sept 11, 1944
~~for~~ at Sea -

Dear Mom,

I got your Vmail of Aug 25, about
a week ago. I don't ~~know~~ where it
came from cause we were at sea but I
sure was glad to get it.

We were running around where it
is ~~supposed~~ to be very ~~hot~~, but I
thought it was a little cooler than
other places where ~~else~~ we have been.

I haven't been where you thought
I was for a very long time now.

It has been raining a lot today and
the flight deck was wet so I didn't
go outside to sleep today.

I was ~~supposed~~ to write a letter
to Jenette a long time ago but haven't
yet. Hope she ~~isn't~~ ~~mad~~ at me. ~~to~~
Has she started back to school yet?
What grade will she be in now.

How is Donnie and David? Are
Donnie's tonsils alright yet?
Don't bother to send me anything
for Christmas. I am not planning
to send anything home. I'll wait
for next year.

Don't worry about me. I am alright
and feel fine. I'll write again soon.

Love Buddy - ...

V Pvin Herwin

September 11, 1944

Dear Mom,

I got your V-mail of August 25 about a week ago. I don't know where it came from cause we were at sea but I sure was glad to get it. We were running around where it is supposed to be very hot but I thought it was a little cooler than other places where we have been.

I haven't been where you thought I was for a very long time now.

It has been raining a lot today and the flight deck was wet so I didn't go outside to sleep today.

I was supposed to write a letter to Jeanette a long time ago but haven't yet. I hope she isn't mad at me. Has she started back to school yet? What grade will she be in now? How is Donnie and David? Are Donnie's toenails all right yet?

Don't bother to send me anything for Christmas. I am not planning to send anything home. I'll wait for next year.

Don't worry about me. I am all right and feel fine. I'll write again soon.

Love,

Buddy

29 AUGUST – UNDERWAY FROM ENIWETOK TO STRIKE PALAU, YAP, ULITHI, MINDANAO, PALMAS, TALAUD, MORETAI AND TO SUPPORT CAPTURE AND OCCUPATION OF PELELIU-NGOBOSUS-ANGAUR AND YAP-ULITHI.

6 SEPTEMBER – LAUNCHED STRIKES AGAINST PALAU, NGOBOSUS.

7 SEPTEMBER – LAUNCHED STRIKES AGAINST NGOBOSUS, ANGAUR.

8 SEPTEMBER – LAUNCHED STRIKES AGAINST KOROR, ANGAUR.

9 SEPTEMBER – LAUNCHED STRIKES AGAINST DIGAS, BUAYAN, CAGAYAN, MAHABA, PADADA.

10 SEPTEMBER – LAUNCHED STRIKES AGAINST PADADA, MALABANG AIRFIELDS.

**Author Note:** The purpose of these strikes was to neutralize the air power of the Japanese during the offensive actions against Moratai, Peleliu, and Ulithi. These locations would be needed as "advanced bases" during future campaigns in the Southern Philippines.

This Navy Recruiting Poster Uses a Phrase from Lincoln's *Gettysburg Address*

# Chapter Thirty-Eight

## Really Busy Pop

Really busy at what? Whenever Buddy uses that term, and he uses it a lot, it means that they have been sending planes to battle loaded with fuel, bombs, and ammunition to destroy the enemy. Sometimes, the planes return from a mission, land, get refueled, guns re-armed, bombs loaded, and take off on another mission as soon as possible. He cannot tell his family what he is really doing because the censors would cut that out of the letter.

Sept 11, 1944
- at sea -

Dear Pop,

Well I hope you had a swell birthday yesterday. I wished that I could have been there to help you celebrate it. I sent a birthday greeting to you the other day but I don't suppose you will get it until you get this letter.

We have been pretty busy as you know. We don't get very much mail at sea unless it is off another ship, but that isn't very often.

It was raining almost all day so I didn't go outside to sleep.

About the last I heard from home was that you were getting your car fixed up. Hope you don't have to bother with the street cars again for a while.

Has anybody moved in the house yet? I understand that a lot of people were wanting it.

Well I'll write again when I can think of something else to write about. Don't worry about me.

Penis Heaven
yours son
Dudds.

September 11, 1944

Dear Pop,

Well I hope you had a swell birthday yesterday. I wish that I could have been there to help you celebrate it.  I sent a birthday greeting to you the other day but I don't suppose you will get it until you get this letter.

We have been pretty busy as you know. We don't get very much mail at sea unless it is off another ship but that isn't very often.

It was raining almost all day so I didn't go outside to sleep.

About the last I heard from home was that you were getting your car fixed up. Hope you don't have to bother with the street cars again for a while. Has anybody moved into in the house yet? I understand that a lot of people were wanting it.

Well I'll write again when I can think of something else to write about. Don't worry about me.


Your son,

Buddy

SEE PREVIOUS LETTER

# Chapter Thirty-Nine

## Promotion to Seaman First Class

Sept 25, 1944
— at sea —

Dear Mom,

I got your letter of Sept 3 a few days ago and sure was glad to hear from you. We don't get very much mail at sea except off another ship once in a while.

I haven't gotten your magazines yet or your candy but I am still waiting.

I get to be seaman first next month. It is $12.00 a month more.

We have been busy the last few days if you read the newspapers.

Why don't you please ask me some questions.

Well how is everything at home?

Well I'll write again when I have more to say.

love
Buddy

✓ Pardin Heaven

September 25, 1944

(at sea)

Dear Mom,

I got your letter of September 3 a few days ago and was sure glad to hear from you.

We don't get very much mail at sea except off another ship once in a while. I haven't gotten your magazines yet or your candy but I am still waiting.

I get to be Seaman First next month. It is $12 a month more.

We have been busy the last few days if you read the newspapers.

Why don't you please ask me some questions?

Well how is everything at home? Well, I'll write you again when I have more to say.

Love,

Buddy

**Author Note:** Some readers might notice that a series of strikes may seem indiscriminate to those who have no idea where those places are. The Navy however, determined these targets through intelligence reports received through reconnaissance flights, on-ground intelligence, reports from underground fighters, *etc.* These reports identified enemy airfields, supply centers, along with air and land defenses that needed to be destroyed prior to offensive actions by our own forces. Frequently, because of these planes' bombing raids, our Army and Marines encountered limited hostile activity from enemy forces defending these islands.

12 SEPTEMBER – LAUNCHED STRIKES AGAINST CEBU AND NEGROS SHIPPING.

13 SEPTEMBER – LAUNCHED STRIKES AGAINST BACOLOD, DUMAGUETE, ALICANTE, MANAPLA, AND COBU.

14 SEPTEMBER – LAUNCHED STRIKES AGAINST .DAVAO, PADADA, MAPANGET, CELEBES, AND DARONG.

15 SEPTEMBER – LAUNCHED STRIKES AGAINST MOROTOI

17 SEPTEMBER – REFUELED DESTROYERS AND CONDUCTED ROUTINE FLIGHT PATROLS FOR FOUR DAYS.

21 SEPTEMBER – *WASP* PLANES FIRST OVER MANILA BAY. CONDUCTED STRIKES BY FIGHTER, BOMBER, AND TORPEDO PLANES.

22 SEPTEMBER – LAUNCHED TWO COMBINED STRIKES AGAINST MANILA BAY SHIPPING AND PORT INSTALLATIONS... *WASP* RECEIVED A 16 MINUTE DIVE BOMBER ATTACK BY JAP "ZEKES, "OSCARS" AND "HEMPS. " *WASP* SHOT DOWN ONE PLANE.

24 SEPTEMBER – LAUNCHED THREE STRIKES AGAINST VISAYAS, NEGROS, AND COBU SHIPPING. EVENING DEPARTURE FOR MANUS, ADMIRALTY ISLANDS, BISMARCK ARCHIPELAGO.

# Chapter Forty

## No Presents for Christmas

Sept 29, 1944

Dear Pop,

I was very glad to get your letter and the funny papers yesterday. I had quite a lot of reading material cause I got mail from Jean and Ruthy too.

I think you have a very good postwar plan but the war still isn't done out here yet.

I have been keeping pretty busy lately. In the mornings I am on a working party to break out stores from the storerooms to eat. & Jis usually takes about all morning.

In the afternoons I go down and help the censors, seal letters and stamp them censored.

not very long ago, I cant say the date, we crossed the equator, so--- they inisnated us into the "Shellbacks Society". & hey really gave us the works. We got hit with rubber hoses, rubbed all over with axlepel grease, got our hair cut, and dumped into a tank of water. It really was a lot of fun but was hard to sit down for a few days.

I sent the ships newspaper to mom the other day. Be sure to read it as it is very interesting.

They passed a lot of men to seaman first class not very long ago. I was in on that so I will get #12. a month more now. It will start the first of next month.

I am not going to send anybody anything for Christmas this year. and I don't expect anybody to send me anything. Maby by next year I'll be home and we can make up for lost time.

as far as going back to the coldroom when I get back, thats where I want to work. They said that I will always be able to come back to the Good Humor Co, and get a job no mater what happens. and thats where I want to work any way when I get out.

Well I want to thank you again for the funny papers. They are help out a lot from going nuts.

I'll write again in a few more days.

your love,

P.S. Did you get my birthday card.

Pervin
✓ Pervin Heuven

September 29, 1944

Dear Pop,

I was very glad to get your letter and the funny papers yesterday. I had quite a lot of reading material cause I got mail from Jean and Ruthie too.

I think you have a very good postwar plan but the war still isn't done out here yet.

I have been keeping pretty busy lately. In the mornings I am on a working party to break out stores from the store rooms to eat. This usually takes about all morning. In the afternoon I go down and help the censors seal letters and stamp them CENSORED.

Not very long ago, I can't say the date, we crossed the equator so they initiated us in to the Shellbacks' Society. They really gave us the works. We got hit with rubber hoses, rubbed all over with axle grease, got our hair cut, and dumped into a tank of water. It really was a lot of fun but was hard to sit down for a few days.

I sent the ship's newspaper to Mom the other day. Be sure to read it as it is very interesting.

They passed a lot of men to Seaman First-Class not very long ago. I was in on that so I will get $12 a month more now. It will start the first of next month.

I am not going to send anybody anything for Christmas this year and I don't expect anybody to send me anything. Maybe by next year I'll be home and we can make up for lost time.

As for as going back to the cold room when I get back, that's where I want to work. They said that I will always be able to come back to the Good Humor Company and get a job no matter what happens. And that's where I want to work anyway when I get out.

Well I want to thank you again for the funny papers. They sure help out a lot from going nuts. I'll write you again in a few more days.

Your son,

Perrin

P. S. Did you get my birthday card?

27 SEPTEMBER – CROSSED THE EQUATOR.

28 SEPTEMBER – ANCHORED AT SEADLER HARBOR, MANUS ISLAND

Buddy's comments in retrospect many years later:

When off duty we could eat, sleep, write letters home or watch air operations. The *USS WASP* would turn into the wind and the cool breeze felt good. Exciting to see airplanes taking off or landing. We would watch the other ships in our task force around us like friendly neighbors. We would look out each other. The cruisers, strong but beautiful, we felt safe with them. One, the *USS Canberra* took a torpedo hit that was intended for us. The speedy destroyers on sub patrol were further out but always on guard. They would refuel from us sometimes. Our own airplanes were high above us on constant watch. The other carriers looked like us. It was almost like seeing ourselves in a mirror except for the different paint patterns. (So the airplanes would know what ship they were to land on.)

# Chapter Forty-One

## General Quarters

When the ship is in dangerous conditions, such as the threat of an enemy attack, all the ship's personnel must be on high alert and in a state of readiness. When this is the case, the captain will issue the command: "**Sound General Quarters!**" Special horns blare and speakers blast the "**General Quarters**" signal. All personnel must move quickly to report to their assigned General Quarters (GQ) duty station. They remain at GQ until the Captain determines that the threat (sometimes battle) is past. This status can last for several hours, many of which could be intensely stressful, emotionally exhausting hours. Imagine the thoughts of the sailors at a quad gun mount who will soon be aiming their gun sights at Japanese *Kamikaze* pilots flying their planes straight at the ship, guns blazing, bombs ready to drop. The Japanese pilots' mission: destroy the ship. The sailors' mission: shoot the planes down before they hit the ship.

Buddy couldn't say this in his letters, but he told me that during "General Quarters," his duty station was on a 5-inch .38 caliber gun mount. He served on the gun crew as they aimed to shoot down attacking enemy planes.

Oct 18, 1944

Dear Mom,

I am sorry I haven't written lately but there just isn't very much to write about.

Read the newspapers but don't believe any Jap propaganda.

I don't know when we are coming back to the states. Only God and the admiral know that. And the admiral hasn't told me.

I got your two packages of magazine and the box of candy. The candy was all gooy but was good and I sure got a lot of reading from the magazines. Please send some more soon.

I was looking my blues over this morning to brush off any mold. I tried some on to see if they still fit. They were a lot tighter than they used to be and looked nice. I guess I am getting fat off this navy chow. I don't know how much I weigh. I haven't weighed myself since I left the states.

Well if I don't write for a while don't worry, remember the insurance.

Love, Buddy

V Pinin Heavern S/C

178

October 18, 1944

Dear Mom,

I am sorry I haven't written lately but there just isn't very much to write about. Read the newspapers but don't believe any Jap propaganda.

I don't know when we are coming back to the states. Only God and the admiral know that and the admiral hasn't told me.

I got your two packages of magazines and a box of candy. The candy was all gooey but was good and I sure got a lot of reading from the magazines. Please send some more soon.

I was looking my blues over this morning to brush off any mold. I tried some on to see if they still fit. They were a lot tighter than they used to be and looked nice. I guess I am getting fat off this navy chow. I don't know how much I weigh. I haven't weighed myself since I left the states.

Well if I don't write a while don't worry, remember the insurance.

Love,

Buddy

**Author Note:** The *USS WASP*, part of Task Force 38 streamed into the Philippine Sea tasked with neutralizing Japanese airbases within operational air distance of Leyte Island where the invasion of the Philippines was planned for October 20.

6 OCTOBER – VERY HEAVY SEAS AND WIND RESULTING FROM TYPHOON. ONE MAN KILLED BY WAVE.

10 OCTOBER – LAUNCHED FOUR COMBINED STRIKES AGAINST OKINAWA AND HAHN JINN.

11 OCTOBER – LAUNCHED FIGHTER SWEEP AGAINST APPARI AND NORTHERN LUZON.

**Author Note:** Formosa (Taiwan), a strategic island off China was also slated for invasion. It became Task Force 38's target for several days. The Japanese Navy made an all-out three day effort to protect (at the cost of over 500 planes) the island's twenty merchant vessels, ammo dumps, and other military supplies. U.S. losses were 79 planes, 64 pilots and air crewman, and non-lethal damage to other task force ships.

12 OCTOBER – LAUNCHED FOUR STRIKES AGAINST TOSHIEN AND TAKAO ON FORMOSA. FIRST PLANES TO HIT FORMOSA.

13 OCTOBER – LAUNCHED FOUR COMBINES STRIKES AGAINST HEITO AND OKAYAMA ON FORMOSA... WASP UNDER ATTACK BY "BETTY" TYPE JAP TORPEDO PLANES ACCOMPANIED BY "ZEKE" AND "OSCARS".OPENED FIRE WITH 5",38 GUNS AND AUTOMATIC WEAPONS. SHOT DOWN FOUR "BETTYS." A SHIP CLOSE BY GOT HIT WITH TWO TORPEDOES MEANT FOR THE WASP.

14 OCTOBER – LAUNCHED ONE STRIKE OF COMBINED FIGHTERS AND BOMBERS AGAINST OKAYAMA, FORMOSA. AT 1841 WASP OPENED FIRE AGAINST "BETTY" TYPE TORPEDO PLANES FROM DEAD AHEAD. WASP RIGHT FULL RUDDER ESCAPED TORPEDO THAT HIT A SHIP BEHIND THEM.

15 OCTOBER – LAUNCHED 57 FIGHTERS TO INTERCEPT APPROACHING ENEMY.. AT 1630 WASP ATTACKED BY 6 – 8 JAP DIVE BOMBERS. WASP GENERATED A SMOKE SCREEN.

**Author Note:** The few days following October 12 were the most tense in the history of the *USS WASP*. There were hours when the sailors were in a status called "General Quarters" because they were experiencing sporadic day and night attacks. After the battle, the *USS WASP* was selected to stay behind to protect two crippled cruisers.

17 OCTOBER – CONDUCTED NEGATIVE AIR SEARCHES FOR ENEMY SURFACE UNITS.

18-19 OCTOBER – LAUNCHED THREE COMBINED STRIKES AGAINST LUZON.

# Chapter Forty-Two

## I Really Don't Know What Time It Is

Once again, Bud complains about time in the Pacific Ocean. To understand why, the reader is referred by to Chapter 30, page 129 for an explanation. At this point, the *USS WASP* is moving from one time zone to another rather frequently. Eventually, the sailors get frustrated and leave their watches locked in their foot lockers.

Oct 30, 1944

Dear Mom,

I got your letter yesterday of Oct 11, and was very glad to hear from you. I also got a letter from you last week but I forget the date on it.

Well we have been very busy the last few weeks as you probably know. I think we will get to go on another beach party in a day or so. Some of the guys went today.

To date I have received three packages of magazines and I sure have enjoyed them, so have a lot of the other boys.

We saw a picture show last night, the first one we have had for a very long time. It was a old picture that I had seen several years ago but I sure enjoyed it anyway.

I received the card yesterday which everybody signed and I sure got a kick out of it.

You asked how tall, heavy, what I looked like now, etc. Well if I look in the mirror at myself I look just about the same to me. I don't know just how tall or heavy I am but I tried on my blues the other day to see if they still fit and they were a lot tighter and fit better.

No I didn't sell my watch, I still have it but I don't wear it because I don't care what time it is. Time doesn't mean anything out here.

The other question I can't answer directly so you make a guess and you will be right.

Love, Buddy.

L Pervis Hawkins

182

October 30, 1944

Dear Mom,

I got your letter yesterday of October 20 and I was very glad to hear from you. I also got a letter from you last week but I forgot the date on it.

Well we have been very busy the last few weeks as you probably know.

I think we will get to go on another beach party in a day or so. Some of the guys went today.

To date, I have received three packages of magazines and I sure have enjoyed them. So have a lot of the other boys.

We saw a picture show last night, the first one we have had for a very long time. It was a old picture that I had seen several years ago but I sure enjoyed it anyway.

I received the card yesterday which everybody signed and I sure got a kick out of it.

You asked how tall, heavy, what I look like now, *etc*. Well, if I look in the mirror at myself I look just about the same to me. I don't know just how tall or heavy I am but I tried on all my blues the other day to see if they still fit and they were a lot tighter and fit better.

No, I didn't sell my watch. I still have it but I don't wear it because I don't care what time it is. Time does it mean anything out here. The other question I can't answer directly so you make a guess and you will be right.

Love,

Buddy

20 OCTOBER – LAUNCHED THREE COMBINED STRIKES AGAINST MINDANAO AND THE LANDING BEACHES OF LEYTE... WASP RECEIVED JAPANESE PRISONER, RADIOMAN FROM DOWNED PLANE.

24 OCTOBER – BATTLE FOR LEYTE GULF TO LAST THREE DAYS.

25 OCTOBER – LAUNCHED ONE COMBINED STRIKE AGAINST SAMAR ISLAND.

26 OCTOBER – LAUNCHED THREE COMBINED STRIKES AGAINST VISAYAS.

29 OCTOBER – RETURNED TO BERTH AT ULITHI LAGOON. PROVISIONED AND ARMED SHIP.

30 OCTOBER – THE POW WAS TRANSFERRED TO FURTHER TRANSPORTATION TO JOINT INTELLIGENCE CENTER.

# Chapter Forty-Three

## Finally, Some R & R

November 1, 1944

Dear Pop,

I have a little time right now so I thought I ought to write to you.

The weather has been a little warm lately and it sure is nice to go outside and lie around in the sun. We sure have been busy lately and now we are taking a little rest. We have seen some picture shows, the first we have had for quite a long time now.

I am feeling fine and hope everyone at home is the same.

I was sorry to hear that your garden wasn't so good this year but am glad to hear that you have some good sweet potatoes.

I hope to be home by Christmas but I don't know what year.

I got the funnie papers you sent and if you have any more I will appriciate them.

Yes, I have been around a lot of places now but I think you are overrating me some. I haven't done anything special.

Well how are you getting along in the back room? Do you still keep your car in the garage or do the other people use it? Drop me a line soon as I would like to hear from you.

your son,
Bud

Pvin Headrin

November 1, 1944

Dear Pop,

I have a little time right now so I thought I ought to write to you. The weather has been a little warm lately and it sure is nice to go outside and lie around in the sun. We sure have been busy lately and now we are taking a little rest. We have seen some picture shows, the first we have had for quite a long time now. I am feeling fine and hope everyone at home is the same.

I was sorry to hear that your garden wasn't so good this year but I am glad to hear that you have some good sweet potatoes.

I hope to be home by Christmas but I don't know what year.

I got the funny papers you sent and if you have any more I will appreciate them.

Yes, I have been around a lot of places now but I think you are overrating me some. I haven't done anything special.

Well, how are you getting along in the back room? Do you still keep your car in the garage or do the other people use it?

Drop me a line soon as I would like to hear from you.

Your son.

Buddy

2 NOVEMBER – UNDERWAY TO STRIKE ENEMY AIRCRAFT, AIRBORNE AND GROUNDED, AIRCRAFT INSTALLATIONS, SHIPPING IN NORTH LUZON.

**F4U Corsairs on the deck of the *USS WASP* with their "gull wings" up.**

# Chapter Forty-Four

## Hot Weather at Sea

Stories of support from the home front were always enjoyed by the crew. For example, wars cost money, a lot of money. One way citizens supported the war effort was buying War Savings Stamps and Bonds every payday.

November 8, 1944
- at Sea -

Dear Mom,

I thought I better write to you since it has been about two weeks since I wrote you last. There isn't very much to say. I am feeling fine and hope you are the same. We have been pretty busy lately but don't believe all the Jap reports.

We will probably get some mail soon I hope I get some more magazines this time. I am sending along another "Waspirit" Hope you enjoy it. The weather is still hot. I guess it is always this way out here.

You mentioned in one of your letters about seeing one of the company trucks (77), well that was Zwick, the old man who lost two sons in airplanes. Remember I told you about that a long time ago.

Well I better sign off now. I'll write again soon.

love, Buddy

Perry Hawkins

November 8, 1944

-at sea-

Dear Mom,

I thought I better write to you since it has been about two weeks since I wrote you last. there isn't very much to say. I am feeling fine, and I hope you are the same. We have been pretty busy lately but don't believe all the Jap reports.

We will probably get some mail soon. I hope I get some more magazines this time.

I am sending along another *Waspirit*. Hope you enjoy it.

The weather is still hot. I guess it is always this way out here.

You mentioned in one of your letters about seeing one of the company trucks (177). Well, that was Zenick, the old man who lost two sons in airplanes. Remember, I told you about that a long time ago.

Well, I better sign off now. I'll write again soon.

Love,

Buddy

5 NOVEMBER – LAUNCHED STRIKES AGAINST MABALACAT, BAMBAN, AND TARLAC. (in the Philippine Islands)

6 NOVEMBER – LAUNCHED STRIKES AGAINST MABALACAT, BAMBAN, AND ON LAGAG AND APPATOR ON LUZON.

8 NOVEMBER – RETURNED TO GUAM TO RELIEVE AIR GROUP 41 AND TAKE ON AIR GROUP 81.

11 NOVEMBER - UNDERWAY FROM GUAM.

**Corsair Planes on the *USS WASP* at Sea**

# Chapter Forty-Five

## Busy at Sea

November 1944

Dear Pop,

    Well here it is november, the time sure seems to go fast. I have been in the navy almost a year now. Hope I'll be out by next year.

    We have been busy out here lately, have you been reading the newspapers?

    How is everyone at home? All well and fine I hope. Are you growing anything in your garden for winter? Has it started raining yet. Out here it has been raining for months, all summer long.

    Will write soon as I would like to hear from you.

              Your Son,
                Bud

Pacific Heaving

November 14, 1944

-at sea-

Dear Pop,

Well, here it is November, the time sure seems to go fast. I have been in the Navy almost a year now soon. I hope I'll be out by next year.

We have been busy out here lately, have you been reading the newspapers?

How is everyone at home? All well and fine I hope. Are you growing anything in your garden for winter? Has it started raining yet? Out here it has been raining for months, all summer long.

Will write soon as I would like to hear from you.

Your son,

Bud

14 NOVEMBER - LAUNCHED **COMBINED** STRIKES AGAINST MANILA BAY AND NICHOLS FIELD.

**Author Note:** The *USS WASP* carries several types of combat aircraft: fighters, bombers, and torpedo planes. When used together, usually fighters supporting bombers, the term "COMBINED is used."

# Chapter Forty-Six

## Censorship

November 18, 1944
- At Sea -

Dear Mom,

I sure was glad to receive your letter of Oct 25 a couple of days ago. Glad to hear that you got the money order. I'll try to write another one soon.

Hazel sent some newspapers saying that the Wasp was in this Philiphine business. It sure seems funny that the newspapers can say that and we can't. If we do the censors just cut it out without batting a eye.

Some guys say that we will be home for Christmas but they don't say which one. I think it will be          if we are lucky.

Well I am feeling fine and working hard. I haven't gotten any more magazines lately but I am still waiting.

How is Unkie getting along, I ought to write to him but I haven't his address will you please send it or ask him to write me a letter and send it. You have mentioned several times that the city is very crowded, why?

Well I better sign off now.        Love, Buddy

November 18, 1944

-at sea-

Dear Mom,

I sure was glad to receive your letter of October 25 a couple of days ago. Glad to hear that you got the money order. I'll try to write another one soon.

Hazel sent some newspapers saying that the *WASP* was in this Philippines business. Sure seems funny that the newspapers can say that and we can't. If we do the censors just cut it out without batting an eye.

Some guys say that we will be home for Christmas but they don't say which one. I think it will be <CENSORED> if we are lucky. Well, I am feeling fine and working hard.

I haven't gotten any more magazines lately but I am still waiting. How is Unkie getting along? I ought to write him but I haven't his address. Will you please send it or ask him to write me a letter and send it.

You have along mentioned several times that the city is very crowded. Why?

Well, I better sign off now.

Love,

Buddy

19 NOVEMBER – LAUNCHED STRIKES AGAINST (San) FERNANDO, LAOAG, SANTA CRUZ, APARRI, TARLAC, CABANATUAN AND LINGAYEN GULF.

**Author Note:** The *USS WASP* continues to support operations to liberate the Philippine Islands.

# Chapter Forty-Seven

## Still Hate to Get Up

November 22, 19.
— At Sea.

Dear Mom,

I got your V-mail letter of Oct 18
yesterday I sure was glad to hear from
you. It's going to be a long war but
if I keep getting mail I guess I can put
up with it a while longer.

There isn't very much news from here
right now about the same. Hazel said
she saw Mrs Rogh the other day. She is
going to get the boy's address for me
so I can write to them.

I am feeling fine and working hard. I
still have that habit of not wanting to g
up in the morning. — But I have to get up
anyway. I guess I will never change.

I just got done writing a long letter
to Hazel so I am just about written ou
I don't want to write the same thing all over
again so if you get a chance see her lette
and get the latest dope / and I do mean
about myself. Merry christmas but don't
send me anything because it will probably m
me sick.
Love, Buddy

November 22, 1944

-at sea-

Dear Mom,

I got your V-mail letter of October 18 yesterday. I sure was glad to hear from you. It's going to be a long war but if I keep getting mail I guess I can put up with it while longer. There isn't very much news from here right now about the same.

Hazel said she saw Mrs. Bogh the other day. She is going to get the boy's address for me so I can write to them. I am feeling fine and working hard. I still have that habit of not wanting to get up in the morning but I have to get up anyway. I guess I will never change.

I just got done writing a long letter to Hazel so I am just about written out. I don't want to write the same thing all over again so if you get a chance, see her letter and get the latest dope. (and I do mean dope) about myself.

Merry Christmas but don't send me anything because it will probably make me sick.

Love,

Buddy

AT ULITHI – SEE PREVIOUS DAY.

The National War Fund was created in 1943, and described by president Franklin D. Roosevelt as "a phil-anthropic federation with three simple aims; first, to determine the nature and the extent of the war-related needs; second, to see that everybody has a chance to contribute to the funds required; and third, to chan-nel the sums raised for its member agencies wherever American help is currently most needed—"to raise enough and on time."

Eighteen agencies were part of the Fund, USO (United Service Organizations) being the most important. During World War II they began the tradition of entertaining the troops abroad, a tradition that continues today. The Fund continued until 1947, well after the war and supported by President Harry S. Truman.

# Chapter Forty-Eight

## Home by 1949?

Sunday Nov 26, 19.
— in port —

Dear Pop,

How are you doing lately, I haven't heard from you ~~for~~ for quite a while now.

We have been pretty busy but I think you have been over rating us.

Not very much news we have been seeing some old movies but they were all right. How about sending some more of those old funnies they sure were good.

I think I'll get to go ashore tomorrow. We swim in our birthday suits and eat coconuts if we aren't too lazy to climb the trees after them.

How are you making out in the house by now? Do you still have your own way and keep your car in the ~~gara~~ garage. I think we will be home by 1949. Maybe a few years sooner. How is your job treating you. Write and tell me about it.

Well I'll write again in a few more days.

Your
Son,

November 26, 1944

-in port-

Dear Pop,

How are you doing lately? I haven't heard from you for quite a while now. We have been pretty busy but I think you have been over rating me.

Not very much news. We have been seeing some old movies but they were all right. How about sending some more of those old funnies. They were sure good.

I think I'll get to go ashore tomorrow. We'll swim in our birthday suits and eat coconuts if we aren't too lazy to climb the trees after them. How are you making out in the house by now? Do you still have your own way and keep your car in the garage? I think we will be home by 1949. Maybe a few years sooner. How is your job treating you? Write and tell me about it.

Well, I'll write you again in a few more days.

Your son,

Bud

AT SEA

**Author Note:** The U.S. Army Air Corps took over the responsibility of providing air cover for troops operating on Leyte, Philippine Islands.

**Radio Communications is Central in Every Carrier Battle Group**

# Chapter Forty-Nine

## Radio Shack

December 5, 194?

Dear Mom,

They gave us these cards to send home so I thought I ought to write this letter to go with it. There isn't very much news we are just sort of resting now. I think I'll get to go on another beach party tomorrow or the next day.

The mail sure is slow comming in. About a week ago a lot of the letters were scorched as if they had been in a fire someplace.

They moved me to the radio shack again. The work is easier but the mid night watches are tough. If I get enough ambition I might go up for third class but it will take time. Maby by the time I come home in about twenty years I'll have a crow on my arm. I don't know how they let this card go but it is a little dope. Well hoping to hear from you soon.

Love,
Bud

December 5, 1944

-on shore-

Dear Mom,

They gave us these cards to send home so I thought I ought to write this letter to go with it. There isn't very much news. We are just sort of resting now.

I think I'll get to go on another beach party tomorrow or the next day.

The mail sure is slow coming in. About a week ago a lot of the letters were scorched as if they had been in a fire someplace.

They moved me to the radio shack again. The work is easier but the midnight watches are tough.

If I get enough ambition, I might go up for Third Class (Petty Officer) but it will take time. Maybe by the time I come home in about 20 years I'll have a Cross on my arm.

I don't know how they let this card go. It is a little dopey.

Well, hoping to hear from you soon.

Love,

Bud

24-30 NOVEMBER – ANCHORED AT ULITHI LAGOON. LOAD ARMOR AND PROVISION SHIP.

1 DECEMBER – UNDERWAY FROM ULITHI.

2-9 DECEMBER - RETURNED TO ULITHI. CONTINUED TO REARM AND PROVISION SHIP.

**Unidentified Squadron and *USS WASP* Support Personnel. Note Bud is on the top row, fourth from the left.**

# Chapter Fifty

## Bomb Duty

Notice the censor hole in the middle of the page.

December 18, 1944
- at Sea -

Dear Mom,

We have been very busy the last few days so please excuse me for not writing sooner. Well I have been changed around again. I am now in the aviation ordnance dept. I work on the ███████████████ and it sure is interesting.

The way it started was that some new men came aboard that had gone to radio school so they ~~placed a lot of~~ it a men to be transfered to other departments. I was one. I asked if I could work with torpedos because, as you remember I went to torpedo school. Well they gave me the bombs but they are pretty nearly the same anyway so I am not complaining.

I like the work very much and we are very busy on days we strike. The rest of the times are pretty free however.

There isn't very much more news. I sent a wasspirit but I guess it will come back because one page had too much information. As soon as I get it I'll take that page out and send it on again.

↳ Lovin Heavens

I think I mentioned before that they took our pictures. They came out good too. I haven't sent it yet because I haven't got a big enough envelope for it. I will try to get one soon and send it off though.

Pay day will be in a couple more days and I have quite a lot on the books now. So I'll draw it all off and send it home.

The mail has been very slow in coming. The last one I received from you was Nov 25, I guess we have a lot waiting for us someplace or on the way.

Well I know I wont see the States this Christmas but ~~maybe~~ maybe next year.

Hoping everyone a ~~Happy~~ Merry Christmas and a Happy New year.

Love,
Bud

December 18, 1944 -at sea-

Dear Mom,

We have been very busy the past few days so please excuse me for not writing sooner.

Well, I have been changed around again. I am now in the aviation ordinance department. I work on the [CENSORED] and it sure is interesting. The way it started was that some men came aboard that had gone to Radio School and they had a lot of extra men to be transferred to other departments. I was one. I asked if I could work with torpedoes because, as you remember, I went to torpedo school. Well they gave me the bombs but they are pretty nearly the same anyway so I am not complaining. I like the work very much and we are very busy on days we strike. The rest of the times are pretty free however.

There isn't very much more news. I sent a *Waspirit* but I guess it will come back because one page had too much information. As soon as I get it I'll take that page out and send it on again.

I think I've mentioned before that they took our pictures. They came out good too. I haven't sent it yet because I haven't got a big enough envelope for it. I will try to get one soon and send it off though.

Payday will be in a couple more days and I have quite a lot on the books now. So I'll draw it all off and send it home.

The mail has been very slow in coming. The last one I received from you was November 25. I guess we have a lot waiting for us someplace or on the way.

Well I know I won't see the States this Christmas but maybe next year.

Hoping everyone a Merry Christmas and a Happy New Year.

Love,

Bud

10 DECEMBER – UNDERWAY FROM ULITHI ATOLL TO SUPPORT OPERATIONS BY STRIKES ON NORTHERN AND CENTRAL PHILIPPINES, TO NEUTRALIZE THE ENEMY'S AIR POWER AND CLOSE HIS HARBORS.

12 DECEMBER – RENDEZVOUSED WITH TASK FORCE AND SET COURSE FOR OPERATION AREA EAST OF LUZON.

14-16 DECEMBER – LAUNCHED FIVE STRIKES OF FIGHTERS AND FIGHTER-BOMBERS AGAINST LUZON AIRFIELDS WITH 500 LB BOMBS AND ROCKETS.

18 DECEMBER – FLIGHT OPERATIONS CANCELED DUE TO HEAVY SEAS. *WASP* WAS WITHIN 33 MILES OF CENTER OF TYPHOON; SUFFERED LITTLE DAMAGE.

**Author Note:** The reader will recognize the countless strikes that are taking place every day by the *USS WASP* and the other aircraft carriers of the Task Force. These are not indiscriminate attacks on enemy positions but planned attacks with a definite purpose and objective. To do otherwise would be very expensive in men, aircraft, and ammunition.

The strikes of 14-16 December were to designed prevent Japanese fighter planes from endangering our landings on the southwest coast of Mindanao.

# Chapter Fifty-One

## Christmas Eve on the *U.S.S. WASP*

UNITED STATES SHIP WASP

December 24, 1944

Dear Pop,

Well how are you getting along lately I haven't heard from you for some time now.

Do you remember that it was one year ago yesterday that I held up my hand and swore after me. I thought it would be over by this time but it isn't and I still am out here.

Well tomorrow is Christmas and it sure is going to seem different. It isn't like Christmas out here, seems months off yet.

I am now striking for aviation ordnance man. It is very interesting and I like the work. We get very busy when we are having strikes but the rest of the time we just loaf around and get tan and study.

I sent one of the ships papers not long ago, it is very interesting.

I don't know what we will have for chow tomorrow but I guess it will be pretty good.

Well how about writing to me soon and letting me in on the news.

My mustache is getting pretty long now. I don't think it is as long as yours yet but it won't be long now.

Well merry Christmas and Happy New Year.

Your Son,
Bud,

I Pierre Harwin

December 24, 1944

(at sea)

Dear Pop,

Well, how are you getting along lately? I haven't heard from you for some time now. Do you remember that it was one year ago yesterday that I held up my hand and swore after me. (my allegiance) I thought it would be over by this time but it isn't and I still am out here.

Well tomorrow is Christmas and it sure is going to seem different. It isn't like Christmas out here, seems months off yet.

I am now striking for aviation or aviation ordnance man. It is very interesting and I like the work. We get very busy when we are having strikes but the rest of the time we just loaf around and get tan and study.

I sent one of the ship's papers not long ago. It is very interesting.

I don't know what we will have for a chow tomorrow but I guess it will be pretty good.

Well, how about writing to me soon and letting me in on the news.

My mustache is getting pretty long now. I don't think it is as long as yours yet but it won't be long now.

Well, Merry Christmas and Happy New Year.

Your son,

Bud

LOG OF WASP ACTIVITIES EVENTS MISSING UNTIL 6 JANUARY.

**Author Note:** Other records I was able to find show that on January 3, 1945, the planes of the *USS WASP* attacked Koryu Airfield on Taiwan with rockets, bombs, and strafing (low, almost ground-level attacks using machine guns). There was no Japanese aircraft defense, so the planes regrouped and returned to attack targets of opportunity such as a cargo train pulling a number of oil tank cars.

# Chapter Fifty-Two

## Movie Night

UNITED STATES SHIP WASP

December 28, 1944

I got your package with all the magazines and candy in it. It came just Christmas day and I sure was glad to get it.

We have been very busy the last few days so please excuse me for not writing sooner. I haven't been on a beach party yet, maybe tomorrow or the next day. We have been busy working loading stuff around.

I am going to save my magazines until we get out at sea again and reading matter is scarce. There is plenty laying around here now.

We have been having some good movies lately. Last night we saw "Since you went away". It was very good.

We had a good dinner Christmas day, Turkey, Ham etc.

I sent a wapsirit but a page is missing because it said too much and the censors took it out.

It has been very hot lately and we were even sweating in December.

Well thats about all for now, I'll write again soon.

Love
Bud

Rein Hawein

December 28, 1944

(at sea)

I got your package with all the magazines and candy in it. It came just Christmas day and I sure was glad to get it. We have been very busy the last few days so please excuse me for not writing sooner. I haven't been on a beach party yet, maybe tomorrow or the next day. We have been busy working loading stuff around.

I am going to save my magazines until we get out at sea again and reading matter is scarce. There is plenty laying around here now.

We have been having some good movies lately. Last night we saw *Since You Went Away*. It was very good.

We had a good dinner Christmas day, turkey, ham. *etc.*

I sent a *Waspirit* but a page is missing because it said too much and the censors took it out.

It has been very hot lately and we were even sweating in December.

Well, that's about all for now. I'll write again soon.

Love,

   Bud

LOG OF *WASP* ACTIVITIES MISSING EVENTS UNTIL 6 JANUARY 1945.

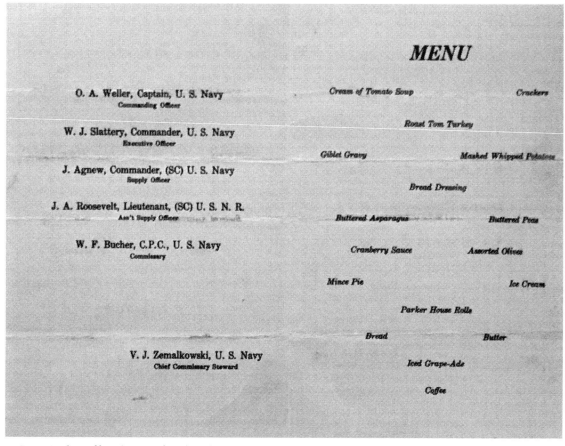

O. A. Weller, Captain, U. S. Navy
Commanding Officer

W. J. Slattery, Commander, U. S. Navy
Executive Officer

J. Agnew, Commander, (SC) U. S. Navy
Supply Officer

J. A. Roosevelt, Lieutenant, (SC) U. S. N. R.
Ass't Supply Officer

W. F. Bucher, C.P.C., U. S. Navy
Commissary

V. J. Zemalkowski, U. S. Navy
Chief Commissary Steward

**MENU**

Cream of Tomato Soup    Crackers

Roast Tom Turkey

Giblet Gravy    Mashed Whipped Potatoes

Bread Dressing

Buttered Asparagus    Buttered Peas

Cranberry Sauce    Assorted Olives

Mince Pie    Ice Cream

Parker House Rolls

Bread    Butter

Iced Grape-Ade

Coffee

**Here is the Official Menu for the Christmas Dinner Aboard the *USS WASP*, Notice that President Franklin Roosevelt's youngest son: J. A. Roosevelt was the Assistant Supply Officer on this Ship.**

# Chapter Fifty-Three

## Short Letter

The *USS WASP* has been sailing into very dangerous territory and has been very vigorous in attacking the enemy. This means the *USS WASP* is not getting any mail sent or delivered.

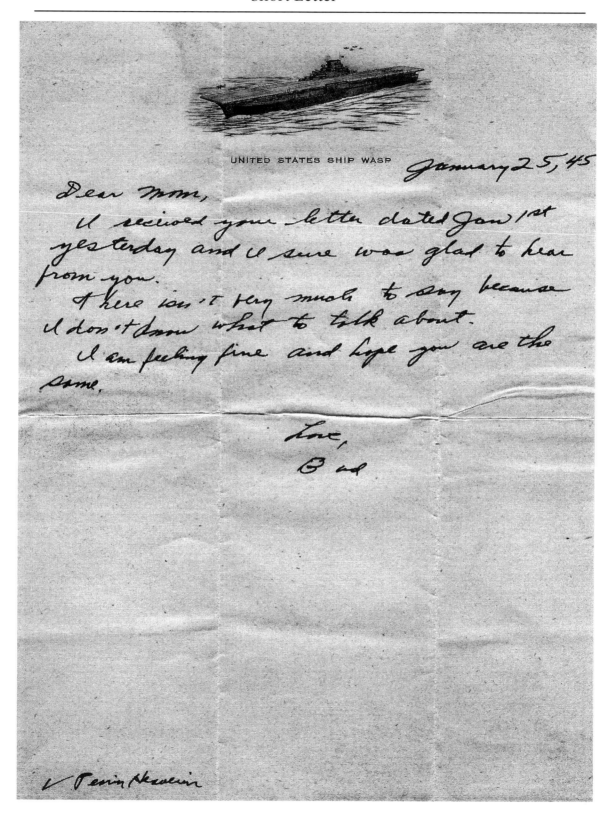

UNITED STATES SHIP WASP

January 25, 45

Dear Mom,

I recieved your letter dated Jan 1st yesterday and I sure was glad to hear from you.

There isn't very much to say because I don't know what to talk about.

I am feeling fine and hope you are the same.

Love,

Bud

January 25, 1945

(at sea)

Dear Mom,

I received your letter dated January 1 yesterday and I sure was glad to hear from you. There isn't very much to say because I don't know what to talk about.

I am feeling fine and hope you are the same.

Love.

Bud

6 JANUARY 1945 – LAUNCHED STRIKES AGAINST LUZON AIRFIELDS.

9 JANUARY – WASP ENTERED SOUTH CHINA SEA THROUGH BASHI CHANNEL EN ROUTE TO ATTACK INDOCHINA.

11 JANUARY – FUELED ESCORTS. MADE HIGH SPEED RUN TO ATTACK AT SUNRISE.

12 JANUARY – BLITZED SAIGON AND CAM RANH BAY.

16 JANUARY – LAUNCHED STRIKES AGAINST HONG KONG AND CANTON AIRFIELDS AND SHIPPING.

20 JANUARY – RE-ENTERED PACIFIC OCEAN UNCHALLENGED AFTER THE 11 DAY SWOOP OF INSOLENCE AND DESTRUCTION AGAINST THE ENEMY.

21 JANUARY - CONDUCTED STRIKES AGAINST FORMOSA AIRFIELDS AND SHIPPING.

22 JANUARY - CONDUCTED STRIKES AGAINST AIRFIELDS AND SHIPPING IN OKINAWA.

**Author Note:** The log of activities reflects only USS *WASP* action. Concurrently, other ships of the fleet are also making attacks on the enemy.

A lot was happening in the war. The role of the USS *WASP* was to contribute the ultimate victory.

# Chapter Fifty-Four

## Dogs on Ship?

Some mail catches up to the ship.

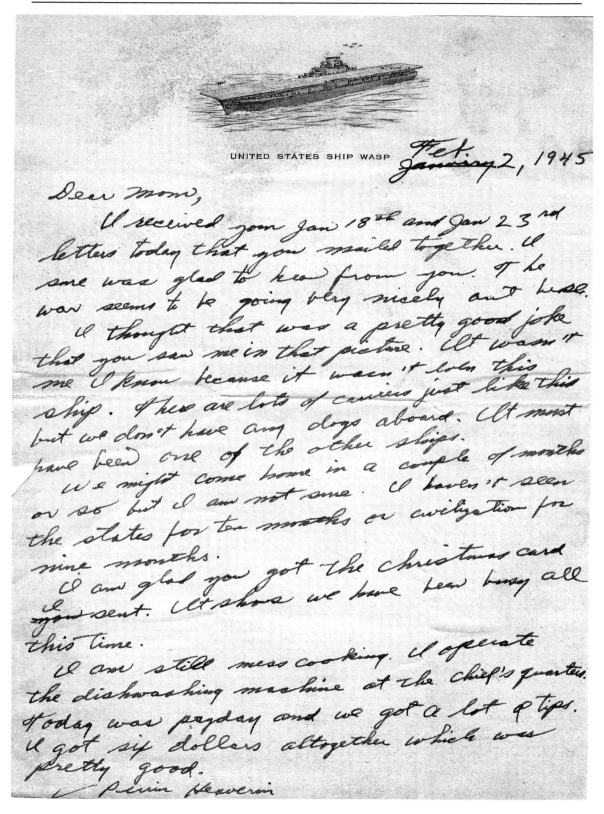

UNITED STATES SHIP WASP Feb. January 2, 1945

Dear Mom,

I received your Jan 18th and Jan 23rd letters today that you mailed together. I sure was glad to hear from you. The war seems to be going very nicely out west.

I thought that was a pretty good joke that you saw me in that picture. It wasn't me I know because it wasn't even this ship. There are lots of carriers just like this but we don't have any dogs aboard. It must have been one of the other ships.

We might come home in a couple of months or so but I am not sure. I haven't seen the states for ten months or civilization for nine months.

I am glad you got the christmas card I sent. It shows we have been busy all this time.

I am still mess cooking. I operate the dishwashing machine at the chief's quarters. Today was payday and we got a lot of tips. I got six dollars altogether which was pretty good.

Sivin Heaverin

February 2, 1945

Dear Mom,

I received your January 18 and January 23 letters today that you mailed together. I was glad to hear from you.

The war seems to be going very nicely out here. I thought that was a pretty good joke that you saw me in that picture. It wasn't me. I know because it wasn't even this ship. There are lots of carriers just like this but we don't have any dogs aboard. It must have been one of the other ships.

We might come home in a couple of months or so but I am not sure. I haven't seen the states for ten months or civilization for nine months.

I am glad you got the Christmas card I sent. It shows we have been busy all this time.

I am still mess cooking. I operate the dish-washing machine at the Chiefs' quarters. Today, we got a lot of tips. I got six dollars altogether which was pretty good.

26 JANUARY – ANCHORED IN ULITHI LAGOON.

4-6 FEBRUARY 1945- OPERATED IN AREA OF ULOITHI WITH OTHER UNITS, CONDUCTED FLIGHT OPERATIONS, MOCK ATTACKS, AND GUNNERY EXERCISES. MARINE CORSAIR FIGHTERS WERE FLOWN ABOARD.

7-9 FEBRUARY – ANCHORED IN ULITHI LAGOON REARMING AND PROVISIONING THE SHIP.

**Author Note:** Constant training is a "must" to be in a state of constant readiness. Missions can be assigned, enemy attacks may come perhaps suddenly and at any time. Be ready!

# Chapter Fifty-Five

## Iwo Jima Invasion

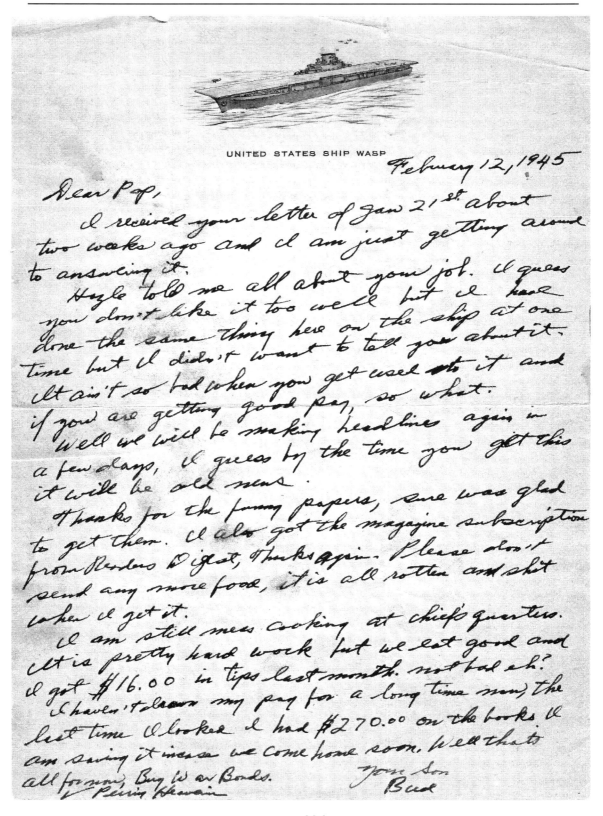

UNITED STATES SHIP WASP

February 12, 1945

Dear Pop,

I received your letter of Jan 21st about two weeks ago and I am just getting around to answering it.

Hoyle told me all about your job. I guess you don't like it too well but I have done the same thing here on the ship at one time but I didn't want to tell you about it. It ain't so bad when you get used to it and if you are getting good pay, so what.

Well we will be making headlines again in a few days, I guess by the time you get this it will be old news.

Thanks for the funny papers, sure was glad to get them. I also got the magazine subscription from Readers Digest, Thanks again. Please don't send any more food, it is all rotten and shit when I get it.

I am still mess cooking at chiefs quarters. It is pretty hard work but we eat good and I got $16.00 in tips last month. not bad eh? I haven't drawn my pay for a long time now, the last time I looked I had $270.00 on the books. I am saving it incase we come home soon. Well that's all for now, Buy War Bonds.

Perin Hawain

Your Son
Bud

February 12, 1945

(at sea)

Dear Pop,

I received your letter of January 21 about two weeks ago and I am just getting around to answering it. Hazel told me all about your job. I guess you don't like it too well but I have done the same thing here on the ship at one time but I didn't want to tell you about it. It isn't so bad when you get used to it and if you were getting good pay, so what.

Well, we will be making headlines in a few days. I guess by the time you get this it will be old news.

Thanks for the funny papers, sure was glad to get them. I also got the magazine subscription from *Readers Digest*. Thanks again.

Please don't send any more food. It is all rotten and shit when I get it.

I am still mess cooking at the Chiefs' Quarters. It is pretty hard work but we eat good and I got $16 in tips last month. Not bad, eh. I haven't drawn my pay for a long time now. The last time I looked I had $270 on the books. I am saving it in case we come home soon.

Well, that's all for now. Buy War Bonds.

Your son,

Bud

10 FEBRUARY – SAILED OUT OF ULITHI LAGOON ON MISSION TO ASSIST IN THE CAPTURE OF IWO JIMA.

The Success of the *USS WASP*'s Attacks on Tokyo Persuaded Army Air Corps General Curtis LeMay to Order Low-Level Firebombing Raids Using B-29s Over Tokyo Similar to What the Royal Air Force Did Over Dresden, Germany Three Weeks Prior and also in Hamburg, Germany in 1943.

# Chapter Fifty-Six

## Toyko Raids

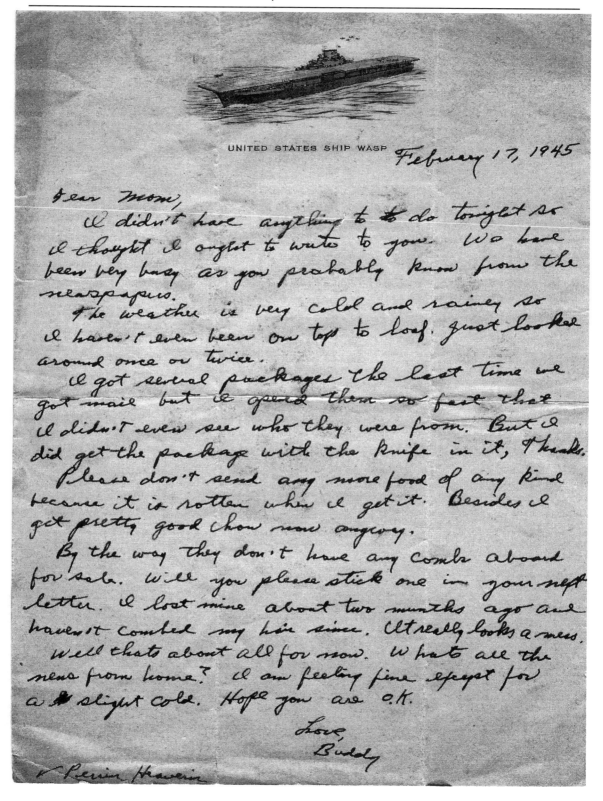

UNITED STATES SHIP WASP

February 17, 1945

Dear Mom,

I didn't have anything to to do tonight so I thought I ought to write to you. We have been very busy as you probably know from the newspapers.

The weather is very cold and rainy so I haven't even been on top to loaf. just looked around once or twice.

I got several packages the last time we got mail but I opened them so fast that I didn't even see who they were from. But I did get the package with the knife in it, thanks.

Please don't send any more food of any kind because it is rotten when I get it. Besides I get pretty good chow now anyway.

By the way they don't have any combs aboard for sale. Will you please stick one in your next letter. I lost mine about two months ago and haven't combed my hair since. It really looks a mess.

Well thats about all for now. Whats all the news from home? I am feeling fine except for a slight cold. Hope you are O.K.

Love,
Buddy

Pierre Heuvin

February 17, 1945

Dear Mom,

I didn't have anything to do tonight so I thought I ought to write to you. We have been very busy as you probably know from the newspapers. The weather is very cold and rainy so I haven't even been on top to loaf. Just looked around once or twice.

I got several packages the last time we got mail but I open them so fast that I didn't even see who they were from. But I did get the package with the knife in it. Thanks.

Please don't send any more food of any kind because it is rotten when I get it. Besides, I get pretty good chow now anyway.

By the way, they don't have any combs aboard for sale. Will you please stick one in your next letter. I lost mine about two months ago and haven't combed my hair since. It really looks a mess.

Well, that's about all for now. What's all the news from home?

I am feeling fine except for a slight cold. Hope you are OK.

Love,

Buddy

16 FEBRUARY – *WASP* PLANES FIRST NAVAL PLANES TO ATTACK TOKYO.

17 FEBRUARY - LAUNCHED ATTACKS AGAINST TOKYO AREA, SECOND DAY OF ATTACKS ON ENEMY CAPITAL. PLANES CAPSIZED ENEMY CARRIER IN YOKOHAMA HARBOR.

**Author Note:** The *USS WASP* lost several planes clearing the skies over Tokyo, but aircraft with bombs were able to hit several aircraft factories in the area. Unfortunately, the bad weather clouds still hid many targets.

# Chapter Fifty-Seven

## We Love the Movies

Notice the top of the letter has been cut off by the censoring officer. The fold lines show there were three equal parts of the page, but now one part is shorter than the others. It probably contained a picture and the name of the ship.

Feb 20, 1945

Dear Mom,

I thought I ought to write to you and let you know how things were. As you can see from the papers we have been busy again.

Say you know that picture you was telling me about, the "Fighting Lady," well we are going to see it. They showed it several times today to small groups and I'll see it tonight.

It is about the first movies we had at sea so we couldn't all see it at the same time.

I'll write again in a few days and tell you how I like it.

There isn't very much news so I better sign off. I am well and feeling fine. Hope everyone is the same.

Love,
Buddy

✓ Perry Heavlin

February 20, 1945

Dear Mom,

I thought I ought to write to you and let you know how things were. As you can see from the papers we have been busy again. Say, you know that picture you were telling me about, *The Fighting Lady*? Well, we are going to see it. They showed it several times today to small groups and I'll see it tonight. It is about the first moves (actions) we had at sea so we couldn't all see it at the same time. I'll write you again in a few days and tell you how I like it.

Playbill the public saw at the local theaters. The ships of the fleet were lucky to see the movie.

There isn't very much news so I better sign off. I am well and feeling fine. Hope everyone is the same.

Love,

    Buddy

**Note:** Morale items like movies and mail were delivered at every opportunity. On occasion, during long deployments at sea, the fresh movie supply ran out so the old ones were shown again, sometimes backward just for laughs.

18 FEBRUARY – LAUNCHED STRIKES AGAINST CHI CHI JIMA.

19 FEBRUARY – IWO JIMA INVADED BY MARINE 4TH AND 5TH DIVISIONS. WASP REARMED AT SEA FOR FIRST TIME, FUELED SHIP.

**Author Note:** The *U.S.S. WASP*'s planes provided air cover and close air support for Marines landing on Iwo Jima.

**A kamikaze splashes near the aircraft carrier *USS Ticonderoga*...**

**These were the stories Bud was starting to hear about...**

# Chapter Fifty-Eight

## The Battle of Iwo Jima Continues

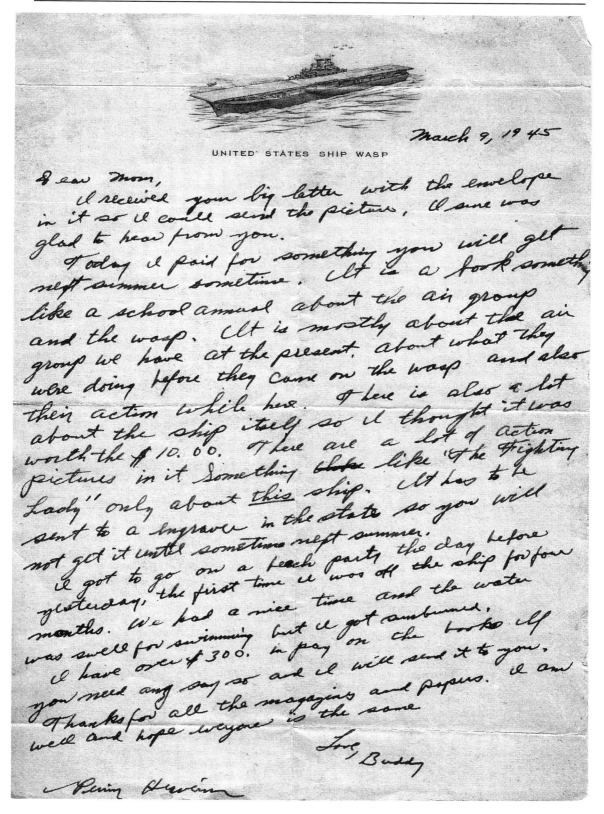

UNITED STATES SHIP WASP

March 9, 1945

Dear Mom,

I received your big letter with the envelope in it so I could send the picture, I sure was glad to hear from you.

Today I paid for something you will get next summer sometime. It is a book something like a school annual about the air group and the wasp. It is mostly about the air group we have at the present, about what they were doing before they came on the wasp and also their action while here. There is also a lot about the ship itself so I thought it was worth the $10.00. There are a lot of action pictures in it. Something like "The Fighting Lady" only about this ship. It has to be sent to a Engraver in the states so you will not get it until sometime next summer.

I got to go on a beach party the day before yesterday, the first time I was off the ship for four months. We had a nice time and the water was swell for swimming but I got sunburned.

I have over $300. in pay on the books. If you need any say so and I will send it to you.

Thanks for all the magazines and papers. I am well and hope everyone is the same.

Love,
Buddy

March 9, 1945

(at sea)

Dear Mom,

I received your big letter with the envelope in it so I could send the pictures. I sure was glad to hear from you today. I paid for something you will get next summer sometime. It is a book something like a school annual about the air group and the *WASP*. It is mostly about the air group we have at the present. It's about what they were doing before they came on the *WASP* and also their action while here. There is also a lot about the ship itself so I thought it was worth the $10. There are a lot of action pictures in it. Something like the *Fighting Lady* only about this ship. It has to be sent to a engraver in the states so you will not get it until some time next summer.

I got to go on the beach party the day before yesterday, the first time I was off the ship for four months. And the water was swell for swimming but I got sunburn.

I have over $300 in pay on the books. If you need any say so and I will send it to you. Thanks for all the magazines and papers I am well and I hope everyone is the same.

Love,

Buddy

21 FEBRUARY – LAUNCHED SUPPORT STRIKE AGAINST IWO JIMA. OTHER SHIPS HIT BY KAMAKAZI PLANES.

22 FEBRUARY – CONTINUED TO SUPPORT TROOPS ON IWO JIMA.

25 FEBRUARY - CONDUCTED TOKYO STRIKES FOR THE THIRD TIME.

1 MARCH 1945 - LAUNCHED STRIKES AGAINST OKINAWA JIMA AND MIYAKO JIMA.

4 MARCH – RETURNED TO ULITHI ATOLL.

14 MARCH – SORTIED FROM ULITHI ATOLL TO ASSIST IN DESTROYING SHIPPING AND DEFENSES IN THE FORMOSA-OKINAWA AREAS. ENEMY AIR ON DECLINE.

*Kamikaze* **Attack on a ship similar to the** *USS WASP,* **the** *USS Bunker Hill*

# Chapter Fifty-Nine

The *U.S.S. WASP* Hit by Kamikaze Bomb

Much Damage, Many Deaths,

The War Comes to Buddy!

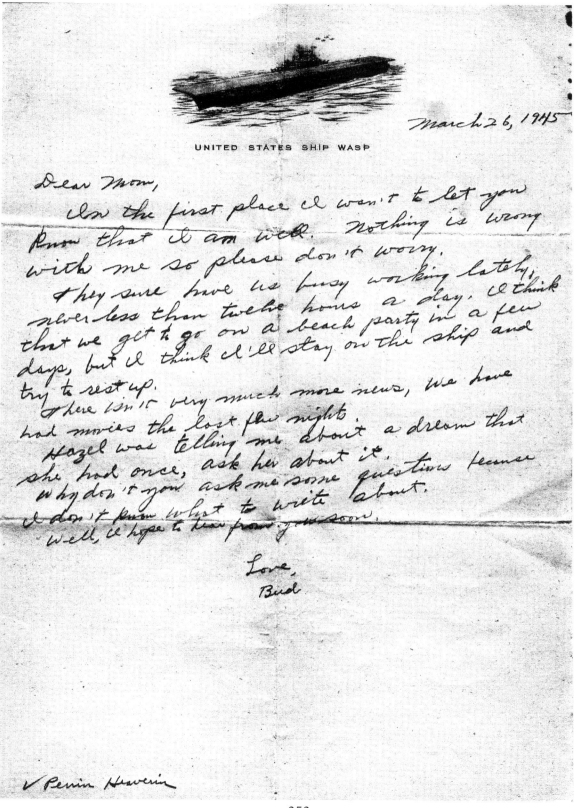

UNITED STATES SHIP WASP

March 26, 1945

Dear Mom,

In the first place I want to let you know that I am well. Nothing is wrong with me so please don't worry.

They sure have us busy working lately, never less than twelve hours a day. I think that we get to go on a beach party in a few days, but I think I'll stay on the ship and try to rest up.

There isn't very much more news, we have had movies the last few nights.

Hazel was telling me about a dream that she had once, ask her about it.

Why don't you ask me some questions because I don't know what to write about.

Well, I hope to hear from you soon.

Love,
Bud

V Revin Heaverin

March 26, 1945

(at sea)

Dear Mom,

In the first place, I want to let you know that I am well. Nothing is wrong with me so please don't worry.

They sure have us busy working lately, never left less than 12 hours a day I think that we get to go on a beach party in a few days, but I think I'll stay on the ship and try to rest up.

There isn't very much more news. We have had movies the last few nights.

Hazel was telling me about a dream that she had once. Ask her about it.

Why don't you ask me some questions because I don't know what to write about?

Well, I hope to hear from you soon.

Love,

Bud

18 MARCH – CONDUCTED STRIKES AGAINST KUNOYO, JAPAN MANY ENEMY AIRCRAFT (BOGIES) IN AREA. WASP SHOT ONE DOWN 70 YARDS FROM SHIP.

19 MARCH – CONDUCTED STRIKES AGAINST RTEBO AND KANOYE, JAPAN. ENEMY AIR ATTACKING ALL SHIPS IN AREA, SOME VERY HARD. AT 0709 WASP WAS TARGETED BY A DIVING "JUDY" THAT RELEASED A SEMI ARMOR PIERCING 540 LB BOMB

THAT EXPLODED ON DECK 3 JUST AFT OF MIDSHIPS. (103 DEAD OR MISSING, 200 WOUNDED). WASP STAYED IN FORMATION AND WAS READY FOR FLIGHT OPERATIONS IN AN HOUR. AT 0832 WASP FIRED AT A "JILL" DIVING AT THE SHIP. WASP EVADED WITH FULL RIGHT RUDDER AND THE JILL CRASHED BURNING 30 FT FROM THE SIDE OF THE SHIP.

20 MARCH – PROCEEDED TO REFUELING AREA. SEVERAL BURIAL AT SEA CEREMONIES WERE CONDUCTED OVER THE NEXT FEW DAYS FOR THE DECEASED PERSONNEL.

24 MARCH – ANCHORED IN ULITHI LAGOON.

25 MARCH - HULL OF SHIP INSPECTED BUT DETERMINED NO HULL DAMAGE.

26 MARCH – UNLOADED AS MANY STORES AS POSSIBLE BEFORE LEAVING FORWARD AREA. WASP ORDERED TO PEARL HARBOR FOR REPAIRS WHEN READY FOR SEA.

**Author Note:** During the week of 17 – 23 March, the *USS WASP* destroyed 14 planes in the air, six on the ground scored two 500 lb. bomb hits on each of two Japanese carriers, dropped two 1,000 lb. bombs on a battleship, dropped a 1,000 lb. bomb on another battleship, hit a heavy cruiser with three 500 lb. bombs, dropped 1,000 lb. bomb on a big cargo ship, and heavily strafed and probably sank a large submarine. The *USS WASP* was under almost continuous attack by shore-based aircraft and experienced several close *kamikaze* attacks... The *USS WASP* gunners fired more than 10,000 rounds (shots) at the determined Japanese attackers.

# Chapter Sixty

## Fun in Seattle

May 16, 1945

Dear Mom,

I'm sorry I haven't written sooner but I have just been too busy. We work every other day and then on our day off we get liberty so I go ashore and just never have time to write.

I have been having a good time in Seattle and I still have plenty of money. Don't worry I have been good.

The weather has been cold and it rains a lot. We always take our peacoats with us on liberty.

For two days last week I went to fire-fighting school. They had built like sections of ships and set them on fire and we went in and put them out. It was a lot of fun but we got all black from oil smoke and one guy got his hair burned.

The ship is really a mess. They have it all torn apart and are overhauling it. They work twenty four hours a day and it sure is noisy and dirty.

It is possible that we may go to San Francisco to get supplies before we go to Pearl Harbor. If so I might get home for a day. I'll write again soon.

Love Bud

May 16, 1945

(in Seattle)

Dear Mom,

Sorry I haven't written sooner but I have just been too busy. We work every other day and then on our day off we get liberty so I go ashore and just never have time to write.

I have been having a good time in Seattle and I still have plenty of money. Don't worry, I have been good.

The weather has been cold and it rains a lot. We always take our peacoat with us on liberty.

For two days last week I went to fire-fighting school. They had buildings much like sections of ships and set them on fire and we went in and put them out. It was a lot of fun but we got all black from oil smoke and one guy got his hair burned.

The ship is really a mess. They have it all torn apart and are overhauling it. They work 24 hours a day and it sure is noisy and dirty.

It is possible that we may go to San Francisco to get supplies before we go to Pearl Harbor. If so, I might get home for a day.

I'll write again soon.

Love,

Bud

1 APRIL – CROSSED THE INTERNATIONAL DATE LINE HEADED EAST.

2 APRIL – MOORED AT FORD ISLAND, PEARL HARBOR. GREETED BY NAVY BAND PLAYING, CALIFORNIA, HERE I COME.

5 APRIL – UNDERWAY FOR PUGET SOUND NAVY YARD. ETA 11 APRIL.

11 APRIL - ARRIVED PUGET SOUND AFTER STEAMING 2,436 MILES FROM PEARL HARBOR. PREPARED TO TAKE ABOARD NAVY YARD PARTY. ANCHORED OFF BLAKE ISLAND TO OFFLOAD AMMUNITION AND THE FIRST LEAVE PARTY. MOVED TO SINCLAIR INLET, BREMERTON, WASHINGTON.

13 APRIL – MOORED AT PUGET SOUND NAVY YARD. MOVED TO PIER 60 PUGET SOUND NAVY YARD.

14-21 APRIL – AT REST ON KEEL BLOCKS AFTER MOVING TO DRY DOCK. BEING REPAIRED IN PUGET SOUND NAVY YARD.

22 APRIL – 25 MAY – WASP IS REPAIRED. 5,000 NAVY YARD EMPLOYEES WORKED ON THE WASP DAILY.

27 MAY 1945 – FLOODED DRY DOCK. THE FOLLOWING REPAIRS WERE DONE.

- THE ARMAMENT WAS INCREASED BY SEVEN .40 CAL QUADS PLUS SIX .50 CAL QUADS.

- OTHER MODIFICATIONS WERE MADE TO THE ISLAND STRUCTURE.

**Author Note:** The "island" structure in the part of an aircraft carrier that rises from the side of the carrier's flat deck.

# Chapter Sixty-One

## No More Liberty

July 18, 1945

Dear Mom,

I got your letter the other day and was very glad to hear from you. But you shouldn't worry about me so much. I am alright and the only reason I don't write so often is because there isn't anything to write about.

We are out at sea again and won't have any more liberty. It is just like old times again and I don't know when we are comming home.

I haven't any more news so I'll have to quit now. Please write soon.

love
Bud

Resin Heaven

July 18, 1945

(at sea)

Dear Mom,

I got your letter the other day and was very glad to hear from you but you shouldn't worry about me so much. I am all right and the only reason I don't write so often is because there isn't anything to write about.

We are out at sea again and won't have any more liberty. It is just like old times again and I don't know when we are coming home.

I haven't any more news so I'll have to quit now. Please write soon.

Love,

Bud

4 JULY 1945 – COMPLETED TRAINING CRUISE.

11 JULY – UNDERWAY EN ROUTE TO ENIWETOK ATOLL.

14 JULY – CROSSED INTERNATIONAL DATE LINE. (NO 15 JULY)

18 JULY – LAUNCHED STRIKES AGAINST WAKE ISLAND.

# Chapter Sixty-Two

## Return to the Pacific

August 1, 1770

Dear Mom,

I thought I better write to you again before you start worring about me. The weather is hot and I sweat just about all the time. There isn't very much to write about we have been busy like we used to. Read the newspapers and find out.

I am well and hope everyone is the same. Please write soon and send some magezines.

Love,
Bud

Penn Heavein

August 1, 1945

(at sea)

Dear Mom,

I thought I better write to you again before you start worrying about me. The weather is hot and I sweat just about all the time. There isn't very much to write about. We have been busy like we used to. Read the newspapers and find out. I am well and hope everyone is the same. Please write soon and send some magazines.

Love,

Bud

19 JULY – ANCHORED AT ENIWETOK ATOLL

28 JULY – WASP PLANES STRUCK YANAGO AREA AT KURE. PLANES ROLLED OVER THE LIGHT CRUISER OYODO ON HER SIDE, AND THOROUGHLY BOMBED AND SET AFIRE BATTLESHIP HAYAUN, CAUSING HER TO BE BEACHED.

30 JULY – LAUNCHED ATTACKS AGAINST HIRATSUKU, FUJISAWA, AND MAIZURU BAY, JAPAN.

9 AUGUST — WASP AIR GROUP 86 STRUCK AIRFIELDS ON HONSHU. ARMY AIR FORCE DROPPED THE SECOND ATOMIC BOMB ON NAGASAKI, MANY ENEMY PLANES SHOT DOWN OVER WASP TASK FORCE. AT 1612 AN ENEMY KAMIKAZE DOVE AT THE WASP AND IT WAS SHOT DOWN, CRASHING ONE HUNDRED FEET OFF THE STARBOARD BEAM. THAT WAS THE LAST KAMIKAZE TO DIVE ON A FLEET UNIT IN WORLD WAR II.

10 AUGUST   LAUNCHED ATTACKS AGAINST TOKYO PLAINS AREA

13 AUGUST   LAUNCHED ATTACK ON TOKYO PLAINS AREA. *WASP* AIR PATROL SHOT DOWN TWO ENEMY PLANES 31 AND 35 MILES AWAY, AND LATER TWO MORE PLANES 41 MILES AWAY FROM SHIP.

**Author Note:** Most air strikes are now opposed by few, if any, hostile planes.

15 AUGUST   LAUNCHED STRIKES AGAINST AIRFIELDS IN TOKYO AREA. RECEIVED WORD FROM ADMIRAL HALSEY THAT JAPAN HAD ACCEPTED SURRENDER TERMS, ENDING 20 1/2 MONTHS OF VERY ACTIVE DUTY IN THE 44 MONTHS OF WORLD WAR II

25 AUGUST  95 MILES FROM SHIKOKU, JAPAN *WASP* RODE OUT A TYPHOON  RECEIVING SEVERE DAMAGE TO THE FORWARD PART OF FLIGHT DECK. DUE TO HEAVY SEAS, THE FIRST 35 FEET OF THE FLIGHT DECK COLLAPSED.

25 AUGUST  –  SEVERE TYPHOON ENGULFED *WASP* AND STOVE IN ABOUT 30 FEET OF THE BOW.  DESPITE THE SHORTENED FLIGHT DECK, WASP PLANES CONTINUED TO FLY MISSIONS OF MERCY — OR PATROL AS THEY CARRIED FOOD AND MEDICINE TO LIBERATED PRISONERS OF WAR AT NARUMI, NEAR NAGOYA.

28-30 AUGUST  CONDUCTED VERY SUCCESSFUL RELIEF FLIGHTS, PARACHUTING SUPPLIES TO PRISONER OF WAR CAMPS.

31 AUGUST   PROCEEDED TO ENIWETOK FOR ONWARD ROUTING TO PEARL HARBOR, THEN ON TO TRANSIT PANAMA CANAL ON 16 OCTOBER ARRIVING IN BOSTON FOR NAVY DAY CELEBRATION

2 SEPTEMBER   V-J DAY

Notice in the following letter, there is no Perrin Heaverin, no censer check marks, no cut-outs, and **No War!**

# Chapter Sixty-Three

## Bringing the Troops Home

For the official surrender ceremony on September 2, 1945, ending the Pacific Theater of World War II, the U.S. fleet was assembled in Tokyo Bay. It was a real show of force. Missing from that armada was the *USS WASP*. Why? Remember on August 25, about a week before, the *USS WASP* suffered severe typhoon damage to her bow and flight deck. The High Command didn't want to show the Japanese any damaged ships in the victorious armada. Thus, the battle weary, but proud *USS WASP* was sent sailing on its way to Pearl Harbor and beyond for repairs. Eventually, it would return to Boston Harbor where it was honored as part of a Navy Day celebration.

January 19, 1945
1946

Dear Mom,

I guess its about time I wrote since it has been so long. I should have written sooner but there wasn't very much to write about so I just didn't.

We made two trips to Europe to bring back troops. The first was to Napoles Italy and the second to South Hampton England. The first trip wasn't so bad. On the way over we took about a thousand Italian P.O.W. We stayed only one day and then came back with seven thousand troops. We took these to Norfolk Virginia. We stayed in Norfolk about 10 days. While we were there several of us went to Washington D.C. We went in the senate and sat in the gallery for a while and then went up in the dome of the Capitol.

We left Norfolk the 18 of Dec for South Hamp and were supposed to be back in N.Y. Christmas eve. We had no troops on the way over and just about 1,000 for the crew so it was a rest for the cooks. But we hit a storm and it tore out several of the steel roller curtains on hanga deck and soaked some of the bunks. So we had to go to Plymouth for repairs. We were there for about

268

a week so they got special trains to take us to London. We had one day in London. On christmas day we left Plymouth for South-Hampton. The next day we picked up our troops and left. We were then supposed to be in new york new years day. about the second or third day out we got into rough weather. It was not uncommon for the ship to list 45° to each side. The troops were all sick and pucking. The flight deck foward began to drop down just the same as it did in the typhone in the Pacific but not as bad. We had been traveling 30 knots but then had to slow down to about 12 the storm carried us farther off its course and instead of getting closer to N. Y. we were getting further away. Finally the storm stopped and we got back on our course again. When we got to new york and got rid of the troops they started taking the lukes out They are fixing the flight deck and giving it a overhaul before it is decommissioned. Three days from now we are going out into the bay and unload ammunition. This will take about five days and then we are comming back in and go into drydock. After that it will be decommissioned. It will be decommissioned in march and then I hope to get shore duty on the west coast. That is if I am not out by then.

Love, Bud

January 19, 1946
(in the Atlantic Ocean)

Dear Mom,

I guess it about time I wrote since it has been so long. I should have written sooner but there wasn't very much to write about so I just didn't.

We made two trips to Europe to bring back troops. The first was to Naples, Italy and the second to Southampton, England.

The first trip wasn't so bad. On the way over, we took about 1,000 Italian prisoners of war. We stayed only one day and then came back with 7,000 troops. We took these to Norfolk, Virginia. We stayed in Norfolk about ten days. While we were there several of us went to Washington D.C. We went in the Senate and sat in the gallery for a while and then went up in the dome of the Capital.

We left Norfolk 18 December for Southampton and were supposed to be back in N.Y. Christmas Eve. We had no troops on the way over and just about 1,000 of the crew so it was a rest for the cooks. But we hit a storm and it tore out several of the steel roller curtains on the hanger deck and it wrecked some of the bunks, so we had to go to Plymouth for repairs.

We were there for about a week, so they got special trains to take us to London. We had one day in London. On Christmas Day, we left Plymouth for Southampton. The next day we picked up our troops and left. We were then supposed to be in New York on New Year's Day.

About the second or third day out we got into rough weather. It was not uncommon for the ship to list 45° to each side the troops were all sick and vomiting.

The flight deck forward began to drop down just the same as it did in the typhoons in the Pacific, but not as bad. We had been traveling at about 30 knots but then had to slow down to about 12 knots. The storm carried us further off course and instead of getting closer to New York we were getting further away. Finally, the storm stopped, and we got back on our course again.

When we got to New York and got rid of the troops, they started taking the bunks out. They are fixing the flight deck and giving it an overhaul before it is decommissioned.

Three days from now we are going out into the bay and unload ammunition This will take about five days and then we are coming back in and go into dry dock. After that it will be decommissioned in March. Then I hope to get shore duty on the West Coast, that is, if I am not out by then.

Love,

Bud

**Author's Note:** Excerpts from the ship's log ceased at the end of the war in the official source document: *History of the USS WASP* (CV-18). 24 November 1943 to 2 September 1945.

The story of the *USS WASP*'s activities continue on Chapter 66: The *USS WASP* after World War II, based upon other resources.

CV-16/A12-1                          U.S.S. WASP

Serial: 1118                                        c/o Fleet Post Office
~~RESTRICTED~~                                      New York, N.Y.

                                                    2 November 1945.

From:       The Commanding Officer.
To:         Office of Naval History, Navy Department.

Subject:    The History of the U.S.S. WASP (CV-18)
            24 November 1943 to 2 September 1945.

References: (a) Director of Naval History Serial CL429
                of 10 August 1945.
            (b) CNO's letter OP-33-J6-JEJ, 118433,
                14 March 1945.
            (c) Alpac 219, September 1945.
            (d) Aviation Circular Letter No. 74-44,
                25 July 1944.
            (e) Aviation Circular Letter No. 101-45,
                11 September 1945.

Enclosure:  (A) Subject History.

        1.      In accordance with the references the enclosure
contains the history of the U.S.S. WASP (CV-18), the seventh
WASP belonging to the United States.  The history begins with
the commissioning of the ship 24 November 1943, and ends with
V-J day, 2 September 1945, East Longitude date.


                                        W. G. SWITZER


Copy to:
        Office of Naval History
        Office of Chief of Naval Operations,
            Aviation History Unit.
        CincPac PUBINFO Pearl Harbor
        History Unit of the Office of Editorial Research



AUTHENTICATED BY

J.N. EGAN, Lieut., USNR.
Ship's Secretary.

# Chapter Sixty-Four

## Anchored in the Bay

Feb. 11, 1946

Dear Mom,

We are now anchored out in the bay. We came out to unload ammunition but we are all through now and can't get back because the tug boats are on strike. This doesn't matter very much anyway because we still get liberty. We are supposed to go into drydock when we get back to town.

I am getting a leave the twenty second for 20 days. I am going to try to get a navy plane home.

There isn't very much more to say so I guess I'll sign off.

love,
Bud

February 11, 1946

(at bay)

Dear Mom,

We are now anchored out in the bay. We came out to unload ammunition but we are all through now and can't get back because the tugboats are on strike. This doesn't matter very much anyway because we still get liberty.

We are supposed to go into dry dock when we get back to town. I am getting a leave the 22nd for 20 days. I am going to try to get a navy plane home.

There isn't very much more to say so I guess I'll sign off.

Love,

Bud

# Chapter Sixty-Five

## Preparing for Civilian Life

Feb. 24, 1946

Dear Mom,

I haven't got my leave yet. They stopped giving them until we get out of drydock. We are supposed to be out on the fifth.

Will you please draw fifty dollars from my bank account and send it to me in a money order. I will need a little more money for leave and I plan to buy some clothes in new york. Also will you try to find out some of the prices of clothes in L. A. If they are cheaper here I might as well buy a few suits and maybe save me some money. I am interested mostly in shirts, pants, suits etc. I can get shoes, underwear, handkerchiefs, etc. in the navy at a good price and I am now stocking up.

I will need a car soon so when I come home on leave I will have to do some shopping. Or I may be better off to get one in chicago and drive it home myself to save shipping cost. I am going to wait a while for the car though until I get discharged.

I will get $300. when I get out and with my bonds and cash in the bank I ought to have a little. Will you also count the bonds and dates on them so I can figure the value and know how much I have in the bank. I should have several thousand and it shouldn't be long before I have a million.

Don't forget to send the money so I'll get it before the fifth.

Love, Bud.

February 24, 1946

(at bay)

Dear Mom,

I haven't got my leave yet. They stopped giving leave until we get out of dry dock. We are supposed to be out on the fifth.

Will you please draw $50 from my bank account and send it to me in a money order. I will need a little more money for leave and I plan to buy some clothes in New York. Also, will you try to find out some of the prices? If they are cheaper here I might as well buy a few suits and maybe save some money. I am interested mostly in shirts, pants, suits, *etc.* I can get shoes, underwear, handkerchiefs, etc. at the Navy Exchange at good prices and I am stocking up.

I will need a car soon, so when I come home on leave I will have to do some shopping. Or, I may be better off to get one in Chicago and drive at home myself to save shipping cost. I am going to want to wait a while for the car though until I get discharged.

I will get $300 when I get out and with my bonds and cash in the bank I ought to have a little. Will you also count the bonds and dates on them so I can figure the value and know how much I have in the bank. I should have several thousand and it shouldn't be long before I have a million. Don't forget to send the money so I'll get it before the fifth.

Love,

Bud

# Chapter Sixty-Six

## The *USS WASP* After World War II

With the end of World War II, the *USS WASP* was decommissioned. The following year, it was moved to the New York Navy Yard for an SCB-27 conversion to allow it to handle the US Navy's new jet aircraft.

With the "Cold War" intensifying, the *USS WASP* was recommissioned on September 10, 1951, with Captain Burnham McCaffree in charge. They rejoined the Atlantic Fleet in November 1951. The carrier spent the following years in the Mediterranean and conducting training exercises in the Atlantic.

**Captain Burham McCaffree**

The *USS WASP* would return to the Pacific in late 1953 where it would operate in the Far East for much of the next two years. In early 1955, it made news when it covered the evacuation of the Tachen Islands by Nationalist Chinese Forces. After completing that operation, it departed for San Francisco for additional upgrades. Entering the yard, *USS WASP* underwent an SCB-125 conversion which saw the addition of an angled flight deck and a hurricane bow. This work was finished late that fall and the carrier resumed operations in December. Returning to the Far East in 1956, *USS WASP* was re-designated as an "antisubmarine warfare carrier" on November 1.

The *USS WASP* would again return to the news when it recovered *Gemini IV* spacecraft on June 7, 1965, at the completion of its spaceflight. Reprising this role later in the year, it recovered both the *Gemini VI* and *Gemini VII* spacecraft that December. The *USS WASP* also recovered *Gemini IX* spacecraft in June 1966. In November, the carrier again fulfilled a role for NASA when it brought on board *Gemini XII*.

The carrier continued to serve in the Atlantic and participate in NATO exercises and missions to Europe until 1971 when the ship was removed from service. The carrier was formally decommissioned on July 1, 1972. Stricken from the *Naval Vessel Register*, the *USS WASP* was sold for scrap on May 21, 1973.

The name *USS WASP* would return to the U.S. Navy's *Naval Vessel Register* a tenth time when a Multipurpose Amphibious Assault Ship (the first of its kind) was commissioned the *USS WASP* (LHD-1) on July 29, 1989. Unlike the last two *USS WASPs*, which were aircraft carriers, this *USS WASP*, this ship was designed to accommodate troops and helicopters. However, as time went on, the *USS WASP*'s roots as an aircraft carrier were remembered as it was re-equipped to handle the F-35B Joint Strike Fighter and the AV-8B Attack Aircraft.

**The Most Recent *USS WASP* (LHD-1)**

## Commendations Awarded the *USS WASP*

**The Phillipine Liberation Ribbon**, with two Bronze stars was awarded to the crew of the *USS WASP* because of the ship's presence in that theatre during the entire campaign.

**The America Theatre Ribbon** was awarded to crew members of the *USS WASP* who participated in the Shakedown Cruise.

*USS WASP* **battle casualties: 106 killed and 200+ wounded.**

## Enemy Aircraft Shot Down by *USS WASP* Gun Crews

June 19, 1944 . . . . . . . . . . . . . 5
September 22, 1944. . . . . . . . . . . 1
October 13, 1944. . . . . . . . . . . 4
October 14, 1944. . . . . . . . . . . 1
March 18, 1945 . . . . . . . . . . . . 3
March 19, 1945 . . . . . . . . . . . 1
August 9, 1945. . . . . . . . . . . . <u>1</u>
Total . . . . . . . . . . . . . . . . .16

Planes from three different Air Groups (12 squadrons) operating from the USS WASP were responsible for the sure destruction of a total of 218.5 Japanese aircraft.

Air Group 14 . . . . . . . . . . . . 151.5
Air Group 81 . . . . . . . . . . . . 42
Attached Marine Squadrons . . . . . . . 6
Air Group 86 . . . . . . . . . . . . <u>19</u>
Total . . . . . . . . . . . . . . 218.5

The Asiatic-Pacific Ribbon was earned by the crew of the *USS WASP*, with Battle Stars for the following operations:

First Star . . . . . . . . Marianas Operation: . . . . . . .10 JUN - 27 AUG 44
Neutralization of Bonins
Saipan
Battle of the Philippine Sea
Guam
Palau - Yap - Ulithi Raids

Second Star . . . . . . Western New Guinea Operation:    15 SEP 44
Morotai Landings

Third Star . . . . . . . Western Caroline Operation: 23 AUG 44 - 14 OCT 44
Capture and Occupation of Palaus
Assaults on Philippines

Fourth Star . . . . . . Leyte Operation . . . . . . . . . .10 OCT to 16 DEC 44
Battle of Leyte Gulf
Okinawa Attacks
Luzon and Formosa Attacks
Visayas Attacks

Fifth Star . . . . . . . . Luzon Operation . . . . . . . . . .12 DEC44 to 16 JAN 45
Luzon and Formosa Attacks
China Coast Attacks

Sixth Star . . . . . . . Iwo Jima Operation . . . . . . .16 FEB to 16 MAR 45
Assault and Occupation of Iwo Jima
Raids on Japanese Empire

Seventh Star . . . . . Okinawa Gunto Operation  .17 MAR to 22 MAR 45

Eighth Star . . . . . . Third Fleet Operations Against Japan
. . . . . . . . . . . . . . . . . . . . . . . . . . . . . . . . .10 JUL to 15 AUG 45

# Prologue

## Perrin "Bud" Heaverin Returns of Civilian Life

Perrin picked up the pieces of his life where he had left off two years earlier. He returned to Alhambra High School and completed the requirements for his high school diploma by attending night school. He was welcomed back at Good Humor Ice Cream Company and was back selling ice cream.

In 1947, he married Lynn Watts. They had a son, Charles, who was born in 1949. Their marriage ended in a divorce. Bud then moved to Orange County and later, had an opportunity to buy a small fruit stand which was the first of his many business ventures. In 1962, he married Eleanor Cusson. She worked with him at their produce stand and later at a firewood yard. They bought and sold real estate for a number of years and were quite successful. They retired in 1987 and continued to live in Costa Mesa. They liked to go to the horse races at Santa Anita Race Track occasionally. They claimed to win enough to pay for their lunch.

Perrin (Bud) Heaverin now lives in Costa Mesa, alone at age 96. His wife Eleanor passed away over ten years ago. His son, Charles now in his 70s, lives with his wife, Marcia, in the nearby town of Vista, California.

Bud is a member of the *USS WASP* Association and, until recently, he was in regular attendance at *USS WASP* reunions held all over the country.

He still drives his car, mostly to the market, church, restaurants, and the senior center once a week to sing.

He enjoys riding the rapid transit trains around the Orange and San Diego Counties with his son, Charles.

Looking for Bud? You'll probably find him on his couch enjoying television reruns of his favorite television programs. Remember these: *Perry Mason*, *Bonanza*, *Rawhide*, *The Virginian*, *Peter Gunn*, *Mannix*, etc.

Yes, Perrin B. Heaverin was a Seaman First Class, a veteran of World War II and part of the crew of the *USS WASP*, a ship that saw action in most of the major sea battles in the Pacific Theater of World War II is taking life easy now. I think he deserves that privilege, don't you?

**Well done, Seaman Heaverin!**

Made in the USA
Middletown, DE
29 March 2022